Buddy MacMaster
The Judique Fiddler

Sheldon MacInnes

Pottersfield Press, Lawrencetown Beach, Nova Scotia, Canada

Library and Archives Canada Cataloguing in Publication

MacInnes, Sheldon, 1949-

Buddy MacMaster : the Judique fiddler / Sheldon MacInnes.

ISBN 978-1-895900-90-3

1. MacMaster, Buddy, 1924-.
2. Fiddlers – Nova Scotia – Cape Breton Island – Biography. I. Title.

ML418.M167M152 2007   787.2'092   C2007-900624-8

Cover design by Gail LeBlanc

Cover photo by Burt Feintuch

Pottersfield Press acknowledges the financial support of the Government of Canada through the Book Publishing Industry Development Program for our publishing activities. We also acknowledge the ongoing support of the Canada Council for the Arts, which last year invested $20.1 million in writing and publishing throughout Canada. We also thank the Province of Nova Scotia for its support through the Department of Tourism, Culture and Heritage.

Pottersfield Press
83 Leslie Road
East Lawrencetown, Nova Scotia, Canada, B2Z 1P8
Website: www.pottersfieldpress.com
To order phone toll-free 1-800-NIMBUS9 (1-800-646-2879)

Printed in Canada

Dedicated to Buddy's parents,
Sarah Agnes and John Duncan MacMaster

Hugh Allan "Buddy" MacMaster.

Contents

Acknowledgements

It is an honour to author this book about one of Canada's most outstanding musicians, Hugh Allan "Buddy" MacMaster. I introduce the voices of many people who have come to know and cherish Buddy. In this process, many people have assisted me in bringing this publication to fruition. I am, however, solely responsible for any errors and/or omissions in this work.

I want to thank members of the teaching and administrative staff at Cape Breton University (CBU) for their ongoing support: Professor Ian Brodie, Chair of the Department of Heritage and Culture; Marlene MacInnes, Instructor and Chair, Department of Communication; Dr. Tony Secco, Vice-President, Academic and Research; in particular, Dr. Arthur Tucker, Dean of the School of Arts and Community Studies; and Dr. Richard MacKinnon, Director of the Centre for Cape Breton Studies and Tier I Canada Research Chair in Intangible Cultural Heritage.

Special thanks to: the staff of the Beaton Institute, CBU (Catherine Arseneau, Jodi McDavid, Anne Connell, Anne MacNeil, Gerardette Brown); Communication and Public Relations, CBU (Irene Khattar); Canadian Broadcasting Corporation Archive for Radio and TV (Doug Kirby and Margaret Isaac); St. Francis Xavier University Archive (Kathleen MacKenzie); Nova Scotia Archives and Records Management (John

MacLeod); Celtic Music Interpretive Centre (Kinnon Beaton and Virginia MacIsaac); Municipality of the County of Inverness (Johnny Cotton); Enterprise Cape Breton Corporation; and the Cape Breton Fiddlers' Association.

I am grateful to the following individuals for their special assistance: Frank MacInnis (Creignish); Betty Matheson (Dominion); Marianne Jewel (Scotsville); Fred White (Big Pond); Denis MacDonald (Halifax); Dan MacDonald (Westmount); Allister MacGillivray (Mira); Joyce Rankin (Judique); and Burt Feintuch (New Hampshire).

To the many people who participated in special ways to make this book possible, many thanks: Danny Graham (Judique); Rev. Angus Morris (Mabou); Mary MacInnis (Creignish); Christie MacInnis (Big Pond); Ronalda MacDonald (Judique); Shea McInnis (Glace Bay); Donna MacKenzie (Christmas Island); Joella Foulds (Boularderie); Burton MacIntyre (Whycocomagh); Joey Beaton (Mabou); Bobby MacEachern (Port Hawkesbury); Francis MacKenzie (Sydney); Doug MacPhee (New Waterford); Jim St. Clair (Mull River); Francis MacDonald (Inverness Town); Sarah Beaton (Mabou); Donnie Little Duncan MacDonald (East Bay); Jack MacNeil (Big Pond); Jackie MacDougall (Judique); Sonny Murray (Sydney Forks); John Donald Cameron (Port Hawkesbury); Jimmy and Margie MacInnis (Mabou); Mary Janet MacDonald (Port Hood); John W. MacInnis (Big Pond); Rev. Eugene Morris (Newfoundland/Collindale); Angela Broley Cameron (Ontario); Lorrie MacKinnon (Ontario); Natalie MacMaster (Ontario/Troy); Linden MacIntyre (Ontario/Port Hastings); Cyril MacInnis (British Columbia/Sydney); John Howarth (British Columbia); Gabe Arsenault (Massachusetts/Belle Cote); Janine Randall (Massachusetts); Tila Lamb (Massachusetts); Barbara MacDonald-Magone (California); Jody Stecher (California); Murdoch "Johnnie Archie" MacDonald (Seattle/Judique); Mark Luther (Colorado); Norman MacDonald (Scotland); Allan MacLeod (Scotland); Liz Doherty (Ireland); and Clan MacInnis (Big Pond).

And thanks to those who supplied photographs: Abbass Studio; SeaBright Productions; Raytel Photography; Bob Martin Photography; Sheldon MacLeod; CBC Still Photo Archive; MacMaster Family Collection from the Celtic Music Interpretative Centre; Public Relations at Cape

Breton University; Shirley Robb, Communications Nova Scotia; Dave Gillis Photography; and Tom Hanson, Canadian Press.

I would also like to acknowledge CBU students Matt MacPherson and Jeff Martin, and Carolyn MacDonald, a CBU graduate, for their technical assistance.

I especially want to thank the MacMaster family – Betty and Kinnon Beaton; Genevieve and Joe Whalen; Jeannie and Gerald Brennan; Lorraine and Jack MacDonnell; Kathleen Beaton; and Alex and Minnie MacMaster for their constant support and encouragement.

To Buddy's wife Marie and their daughter Mary Elizabeth MacInnis and their son Allan, thanks for your guidance and support.

I also want to acknowledge and thank Pottersfield Press for their belief in this book: Lesley Choyce, Julia Swan, Peggy Amirault and Gail LeBlanc. I appreciate your dedication and professionalism in guiding me throughout this publication process.

Finally, thank you, Buddy, for your patience, your music, and for just being "Buddy."

Sheldon MacInnes
Lecturer/Researcher
Celtic Music
Cape Breton University

Buddy MacMaster as he enjoys playing for Cape Breton square dancers.

Four on the Floor

---

*I always try to play lively music that is good for dancing. I like to
see people on the floor dancing, having fun ... feeling happy ... and
that's part of my enjoyment ... At dances I see people with smiles
on their faces ... so that's part of my reward.*

– Buddy MacMaster

It's Thursday night at the Glencoe Mills Hall and the bow arm of Cape
Breton fiddler Buddy MacMaster is "in full drip." He cradles his fiddle,
rendering his signature medley of jigs. His eyes are closed, as he appears
to enter a spiritual trance, giving his full attention and concentration to
the music. His body moves to every tune and to every note as they bond
to transmit a music that is as gentle, inviting and persuasive as it is
unyielding, gritty and rigorous. The stage is set and Buddy's familiar sil-
houette propels the music for the dancers on the floor. The perspiration
seeps down his forehead and across his face from the intensity of his
performance, one that is matched only by the collective energy from the
dancers who are now spread throughout the hall, front to back, focused
on their footwork and Buddy's wonderful lively music.

The small platform at the far end of the hall where Buddy is seated is barren and without frills. A dim light is perched overhead and the small twelve-inch fan that sits on a small table nearby does little to make things cool for him. He knows that a grueling evening awaits him and being fit is a prerequisite. He is robust and athletic in appearance. He has held this position on the typical dance hall stage for several decades. He always looks the same – so agile and so nimble. His form is seemingly ageless. He is wearing his usual crisp white shirt, a tie, dress slacks and black shoes that show a bright polish despite the thumping they have endured to the beat of his music. If Buddy's shoes could talk about their travels, they would shine in ways like no other shoes could.

Earlier that summer evening, Buddy arrived at the dance hall before the patrons. He put his modest sound system in place. He has already worked a full shift this day at a CN station somewhere in Inverness County. The evening is perhaps the second, or third, or even the fifth dance that week for Buddy. It is ten o'clock. He knows that morning will come quickly and then it's back to CN. For now, however, a mission awaits him.

To Buddy's right is a lone pianist, his only accompanist for the evening, who sits in anticipation. The pianist leans with one elbow resting on the small ledge that extends beyond the white keys while a hand grips the chin. The two musicians share an exchange about a tune or a happening in the community. But momentarily, Buddy MacMaster's dance music will permeate the crowded hall, a former one-room school that is located in a secluded woodlot.

The pastoral setting is any rural community in Inverness County. The parking space is crowded. Vehicles are lined two and three abreast bearing license plates from many different places in North America. People are making their way toward the narrow steps leading into the hall. The music can be heard drifting from inside, through a series of small open windows that provide the illusion there will be a way for some fresh air to circulate. But it is only an illusion and it will not matter anyway. From outside, you can now hear Buddy's bow, ever so slowly gliding meticulously over the strings as he prepares to tune the fiddle. He adjusts the tuning; it must be perfect. The routine indicates he is near ready. He begins a tune. It seems that Buddy's music, his opening jig, is in full flight from the very onset – in fact, it is.

The dancers then quickly make their way across the hardwood floor from the wooden benches and from the crowd standing at the back, near the canteen. The invitation to someone from the crowd to partner for a square set is extended and the partnership is secure for the three figures of the set. Together – complete strangers or casual acquaintances or close friends – they move as near to the stage as possible. They want to hear Buddy's music loud and clear and to begin an evening of fun like no other. In terms of physical activity, it's like an extended workout at the Y.

Within moments, there is a display of fancy jig steps. Later, the intricate reel steps will follow. Individual style and innovation are always present. The type of footwear is optional and everything goes – sneakers, sandals, workboots, soft leather shoes, and beach attire. You name it and it's on that floor before the evening is finished. Clothing consists of casuals for men and women. Some are decked out nicely – ready for church. But there is a wide display of sweatshirts, tank tops, walking shorts, and different T-shirts that flash a lengthy list of American states, Canadian regions and slogans such as Been There, Done That, Got the T-Shirt.

Locals, visitors and tourists participate in this weekly drama – for some, it's a nightly routine. All shapes and sizes and all ages are involved. Among the dancers are those new to the scene and if the apprentices are not on their toes, they may quickly be pushed to the back of the hall. As for the veteran dancers, they know exactly what to do to ensure they have a good time. The locals know how to secure a good spot on the dance floor.

As the dance floor fills, the crowd will absorb some of the sound, so positioning on the floor is important even with the use of modern sound systems. For some, eye contact with Buddy is important. This is important for Buddy, too. The dancers will try to hold their spot as the circle grows with couples who want to join the initial circle – the first figure of the set. This routine is timeless. It applies to Buddy's most recent dance settings as it did when he first began playing at dances.

An ideal number for a square set is four couples whether the dance is in Inverness, Glendale or Glencoe Mills. But there may be as many as ten or twelve or more couples in the typical first figure of any set. At some point, the initial circle divides and sometimes again even while the music continues. The exercise is rather unplanned. The goal is to arrive at a reasonable number of couples within each initial first figure. The ultimate objective for some, however, is to remain in a full set of good dancers and near the stage. The good dancers will gravitate toward the music and more good dancers; and among these dancers, timing is imperative.

The jostling for a spot on the floor among the dancers is now common in the absence of the old-time prompters, the individuals who called the sets and kept the number of couples in the set to four, or else! In *The Clansman*, Buddy recalls, "Then there was more concern about how many couples were in a set. The fifth couple was not always so welcomed. It has changed a bit today, and you can see many couples in a set and that means the fiddler has to play much longer to finish a set. It's tiring, but I always seem to have the stamina to get through."

With or without a prompter, however, Buddy's music keeps flowing and the three-figure sets continue throughout the evening. As the evening unfolds, the dancers progress into their own realm in mind, body and spirit. Their rhythmic magic is fuelled by heart and driven by passion. Buddy and the dancers are one in time and space. The dancers' footwork or freestyle steps are representative of the styles still nurtured in Mabou, Judique, Creignish, Troy and further afield. These steps are passed along through the jigs and the reels from one generation to the next. The scene is timeless and ageless.

Buddy MacMaster will take his music and the dancing to a higher level of intimate joy and down-home nostalgia, and together they render one of the oldest forms of building community known to this Highland culture. This community is one of deep passion for the music, song and dance that arrived with the early Scottish pioneers who settled the area. They knew hard work, but they also knew how to enjoy life. Emily Addison, while studying at Trent University, writes in her undergraduate thesis about the dance halls' atmosphere: "The sense of community that is created within the dance halls of Inverness County is extremely powerful." And so it is. For the three to four hours at a dance, Buddy's music is remarkable and continual. The dancing is dynamic and energized. The tradition continues.

Francis MacDonald is from Inverness town. He too is an excellent exponent of the music, song and dance of the Gael. He shares this memory: "The first time I ever heard Buddy playing – in public anyway – was in 1949 at a dance at the Labour Temple Hall in Inverness. In those years, of course, we'd all be waiting for the [weekly] dance. A bunch of us [would] get together and go up near the front of the stage when Buddy was playing ... There were several of us there that were pretty experienced square dancers and we'd ask for a particular tune on the second figure. I can remember that – a nice jig – and everybody seemed to like it ... We'd step-dance, of course, through the last figure ... always near the front of the stage so that you could enjoy the full music. But Buddy was just the same then as he is now ... I mean he hasn't changed in his mannerisms or his gentlemanliness."

Now fast forward. It's the new millennium – over fifty years later. Peter Murphy describes the sense of mystique at a Buddy MacMaster dance. The setting is Glendale. He illustrates how someone can be so close and yet so far from the music. Peter is a well-known photographer from Antigonish – across the causeway that links Cape Breton with mainland Nova Scotia. Through his company, SeaBright Productions, he has produced several excellent videos featuring Buddy MacMaster. In an article he prepared for the Summer 2000 issue of *The Cape Bretoner*, Peter recalls that he attended the 1973 Scottish Fiddle Festival in Glendale. He had not been around "the music" before then but he did hear it on radio occasionally. He writes, "We ventured into the church hall, where almost instantly the music, the atmosphere, or God knows what, propelled me into my first ever square set. As music filled the air ... I was hooked. I didn't realize it then, but I had just come under the spell of Buddy MacMaster and Cape Breton fiddle music."

Then there are those who are always close to the music and who grew up with it. Sarah Beaton who, along with her husband Raymond, both active members of the Mabou dance scene, often frequented Buddy's dances and would not have been born when Francis MacDonald attended that dance in Inverness in 1949. Sarah recalls, "We'd follow Buddy's music around the area. When he was most active, we'd go almost every night of the week during the summer. He was in the different communities. There isn't a place that we'd miss. It's great to get the good dancers together and near the music at the stage and dance away. It's still that way. There's nothing like it."

Fred White from Big Pond recalls his reaction to his first Glencoe Mills dance in August 1973. He had left home for the two-hour drive to Glencoe Mills. He remembers, "Then the magic occurs! Within ten minutes, as Buddy starts to play, the hall seems to fill with a crowd of people both young and old. Within minutes, the floor seems completely filled with sets. As I witnessed this, I wondered to myself where have all these people suddenly come from? Is Buddy a magician who, with the simple act of drawing the bow across the strings on the fiddle, makes the spruce trees turn into people who fill the hall to capacity?

"I wondered about the tourists attending for the first time – what would their reaction be? Do they think they have stumbled upon some Cape Breton version of *Brigadoon*, a magical place in the middle of the countryside that springs to life every Thursday night from June until early September? What the tourists will see for certain is that there is no doubt these people came to dance and not one tune will be wasted!"

For a square dance, Buddy selects tunes to accommodate the dance style of jigs and reels. The sheer number of tunes he plays at a dance is staggering. One square set consists of three figures. In the first figure, the jig, he will play eight to ten jigs twice over. In the second figure, also a jig, he will play eight to ten different jigs, again twice over. In the third figure, the reel, he will play as many as twenty reels twice over. Buddy's repertoire is awesome.

This is Buddy's routine for just one set only (the three figures). Buddy will play as many as eight sets per dance. In between some sets, he will play a slew of strathspeys and reels for the many step-dance soloists who will line up to perform during a brief interlude to allow the square dancers to catch their breath. Intermission, you ask? What's that? The only item that might remotely resemble an intermission is when Buddy invites a pianist from the dance floor to give his accompanist a break. As the switch is made, Buddy gets a wee moment to check his tuning. Then he is back at it. Over the course of a typical dance, Buddy can render hundreds of tunes with precision timing and impeccable correctness for a single evening's dance – all from memory. This is Buddy MacMaster – at his best.

Buddy MacMaster is now over eighty years of age. Although he no longer has the legendary endurance and stamina he once had, he will perform still in public at concerts and special events that highlight a celebration of someone's life. He must. This is what his life is about.

By 2006, there was growing anticipation of a huge ceilidh to honour Buddy's retirement from public performance. The talk was that Buddy might want to pack it in – not a very pleasant thought for his fans and many admirers. However, to this day, Buddy continues to perform and the magic is still there.

Centre Stage

I have known Hugh Allan "Buddy" MacMaster since the 1960s. I first met him while he was playing for a square dance in Big Pond at the old parish hall. I would have been about twelve or thirteen but not too young to be at the dance. It was common at that time to have young and old attend local dances. I had even known Buddy's music for several years before that, as I would hear his homemade and studio recordings often on CJFX radio. I understood that his music was special. I had acquired a particular interest in his playing, having been acquainted with the music from a very early age. My father, Dan Joe (1922-1991), and my mother, Christie (b. 1927), had always spoken highly of Buddy. My father was also a celebrated fiddler, and he had a wonderful respect and admiration for Buddy's music.

My father had arranged for Buddy to perform at that Big Pond dance. Since then, I have attended many dances and concerts in Cape Breton and away where Buddy has performed over the years. I had the pleasure, as well, to be in his company when travelling to a range of events involving the music.

In 2004, I made plans to attend a concert at the Savoy Theatre in Glace Bay to see Buddy perform. I knew he had not been feeling well, as he had just been discharged from the hospital. As for the preparation for his performance that evening, I believed he would have no problem engaging his familiar practice. That is, on his two-hour drive from Judique, he would decide on an opening march. Then he would have a strathspey or two in mind to follow. From that point, he would then allow his intuition to determine the rest of the medley and thus he would retrieve any number of additional selections from the vast repertoire he had accumulated in his lifetime. There was never any question that he could access tunes easily and quickly. And at a concert performance, where he would be among other artists who would help carry the evening, Buddy would be relaxed and enjoy the occasion. But this performance was to be different, as I was soon to discover.

Near the halfway point in the evening's program, Buddy was invited to perform his solo. I remember the moment clearly. He was introduced. He sat on a chair on stage as he acknowledged the audience – a full house. Some might sense this could be the last performance for Buddy at the Savoy.

Before playing, Buddy did something I had not seen him do before. He reached into his pocket and pulled out a small piece of paper. He fumbled it around in his free hand, trying to unfold it so he could read the information he had prepared and still hold the fiddle and bow in the other hand. He reviewed the note carefully and then explained his choices to open the set and added, "We'll see what else follows." He had often spoken that phrase on occasions like this. There was a huge chuckle throughout the audience. To read the titles of the introductory tunes in the medley from the piece of paper first was unusual. It was not Buddy's style. I realized that perhaps he needed to actually see the opening titles just moments before playing in order to set the recall for the medley. It was getting that first tune or two etched in his mind and then he would be on his own. The piece of paper was his prop.

He began to play. The music was wonderful. He finished his first slew of tunes. Upon completion, he received a standing ovation. He had remained seated, as he had been instructed earlier by the producer to perform two sets. Before beginning his second set, he took the note from his pocket and again read aloud the titles for the first couple of tunes. He began playing, as announced, a series of old strathspeys. Some dandy reels followed. Upon finishing, he received another standing ovation. He thought that set would satisfy the audience fully. But not so.

In a concert where one shares the stage with a litany of other performers, this is sometimes a concern for artists and organizers. In Buddy's case, what happens if the audience does not let him go? What happens if they want him to remain on stage all evening? These questions were no doubt looming among those in charge. Some of the artists backstage were likely wondering how they might top this performance. Would they even try? As for the audience, it had been very engaging and Buddy exhibited his usual humble manner. The expression on his face said it all – why all the fuss? But that genuine concern about Buddy's possible retirement made the audience want to hear as much as possible. So, "let's get all we can" was the prevailing sentiment. After all, most of the audience was from Sydney and Glace Bay and they might not have the opportunity to see him again – unless they went all the way to Judique or Mabou. He remained in the spotlight for his third medley of tunes.

Up to that point, Buddy was rendering his music in his familiar effortless fashion. His recall, with the use of the small prop, and his delivery were great. No problem. To begin this third round, he would put himself in an even more challenging moment with respect to a particular tune. In so doing, however, he demonstrated to me a great public performance, as usual.

From his chair, he looked at the audience and he spoke into the microphone. He explained that he appreciated the wonderful response to his music. He also indicated he would play the additional set but then he would move away from the stage so others could perform. Then he announced he had a certain tune he wanted to play – a new jig. He had received the tune from his niece, Andrea Beaton, a few days ago. Buddy explained she had written the tune for him and he was not certain exactly what she had in mind as a title. He paused. There was silence. Then he exclaimed with a hearty laugh, "I guess it will be 'My Uncle Buddy.'" The audience joined in the laughter. I was focused on another matter.

When he announced he would play the new tune, I had instantly wondered whether that was a good idea. How would he recall a new tune at this point in the evening? Perhaps he had not played it in public before. As usual, he did not have the sheet music with him on stage.

And presumably, he had not anticipated the need for a third medley. The music to all the tunes he would play that evening, including the new jig, were at home. Given the newness of this composition, would knowing the likely title and the composer suffice to help him recall the actual tune? Although this is a performer whose repertoire is seemingly endless, as he had learned a ferocious volume of tunes with several thousand put to memory, I was concerned.

I remember being in Scotland with Buddy in 1979. We were doing a sound test for the BBC. They were to record a session of music with musicians from both sides of the water taking part. The technician asked Buddy if he would play his fiddle to start the procedure for checking audio levels. Without hesitation, Buddy tuned his fiddle. Then, he started playing the old favourite, "*Tullochgorum.*"

In the world of great Scottish music, this is a masterpiece and it would allow any technician to get the full range and depth of the "Gaelic sound and flavour" in the music. James Scott Skinner, Scotland's King of the Strathspey, would have been pleased with Buddy's choice. Needless to say, it is a wonderful piece of music for listening and, in the Cape Breton tradition, for dancing, but it is an extremely difficult tune to play. Usually it takes even the more competent musician a considerable time to warm up to play the tune. Buddy drew the instant attention of everyone who had gathered for rehearsal that afternoon and, in that brief moment, validated his remarkable reputation as a master fiddler that had already preceded him to Scotland. And that was just during a sound test. It was a great moment in Buddy's performances.

Now, back to the Savoy in 2004. Buddy sat and gently raised his fiddle, giving his wrist upon which he rested the instrument a nudge so as to move the shirt cuff away. He began to lower his bow ever so carefully. The bow had not yet touched the strings. And, at that moment, I feared the worst. Was he now in a situation that would possibly place him in an awkward predicament? Perhaps he was not certain that he had the tune foremost in his mind. Yet, earlier, in a few words, he had already given high praise to the tune's composer. So he had already set the stage for the performance. Now he had to deliver. Could he retrieve that new tune from all that was stashed away in that bank of aural and written music?

I waited for what seemed like an eternity and yet was only a few seconds. I wondered if there were others in the audience who even noticed that, for a moment, he appeared to be struggling and searching for that tune. Could he find that first bar, the first two or three notes even? That's all he needed to allow the full tune to emerge. I knew that. But could he do that this evening? I wondered.

I watched from my front row seat and took note of the expression on his face. He closed his eyes ever so tightly. I watched as he seemed to concentrate intently. In retrospect, it was marvelous to see. He was alone and all eyes were upon him. Yet he was so well focused. Slowly, he lowered the bow and touched the strings. I was still not convinced he had the tune. Then, in a wink, he began to play – the new jig. (I had heard it the week before when Andrea Beaton, the composer, played it at a dance in Mabou.) He had retrieved it and I was so taken aback. I felt a profound sense of emotion and relief. Silently, I cheered him for having retrieved the tune. He played it very well, of course. Several other jigs were part of that medley, too. Then I began to wonder why I even doubted whether he could flick the tune seemingly from the air. Again, Buddy received a standing ovation as he completed his final set of the evening. He gave his usual wave of the bow and exited the stage. I was genuinely astounded he was able to give that performance under the pressure of playing before a live audience, in a concert setting, and not feeling so well. This was the touch of real professionalism. It was truly a remarkable moment. His passion and his will to perform were all intact.

In 2006, I telephoned Buddy in late June. He explained he was not feeling the best that particular day and indicated he may have to revisit his doctor to have his medication checked. Only a couple of days later, I received word that he had been hospitalized. There he remained for two weeks. In July, he was discharged and most assumed he would take the summer to get some rest. Not so! He was no sooner home when he packed his fiddle and made his way to the church in Creignish. He had promised his good friends Frankie and Mary MacInnis that he would play at their son's wedding. And so he did, just as he had some thirty-four years earlier when he played at Frankie and Mary's wedding. He made his way to the church in Antigonish and later that same day returned to Cape Breton to perform at a dance in Glendale.

Also in July 2006, he went to Louisbourg – on the other side of the island – to play at a concert and that same weekend played at a function in Inverness before travelling to Broad Cove to play. Throughout August, he gave many other performances. Frankie MacInnis shares a memory of one of those August performances. "In August 2006, Buddy asked me to accompany him to the western end of Prince Edward Island to the Atlantic Fiddlers Festival. He was among fiddlers from P.E.I., New Brunswick, Magdalen Islands and Quebec. He was treated like a rock star, not only by the audience but also by the other fiddlers. He got a standing ovation when he came on stage and again at the end of every set he played. After his performance, he was besieged for autographs. On Sunday morning, I came downstairs and the landlady at the bed and breakfast where we stayed lamented that she would not be able to attend the festival to hear Buddy play. I informed Buddy, who promptly brought forth his fiddle and gave her an impromptu session at her house. Soon, the other visitors came down and were treated to a wonderful performance."

Frankie's story validates that there was simply no stopping Buddy MacMaster, and Buddy's anticipated retirement from public appearances is on hold.

Buddy's years of music represent the stuff from which legends are made. To try and grasp some insight into this phenomenon may not be possible in a single publication from one person. In this book, however, I will attempt to highlight not only Buddy MacMaster's musical experience, but also Buddy, the wonderful person – his character, his personality, and his Christian family and community values that are so integral to his music.

This book briefly explores the lifestyle that he lives and has lived, not to judge but rather to try and understand. I will look at Buddy in the context of his most determined goal as a musician – to be a great dance player. That goal was achieved after a longstanding adherence to the full depth and range of the music tradition of Cape Breton – as a young learner first and then as a fully matured performer. He is a wonderful session and concert musician, too. He was and is a master soloist. The skill set is different from what's required for dance play performances. To excel at both, in the Cape Breton tradition, is the mark of a very gifted violinist/fiddler. So many superb fiddlers can shine so well in one but not both. In the final analysis, I'll outline how Buddy MacMaster not only adheres to the old-time music tradition but how he defines that tradition and how he has set the stage for future generations. And I do this to enable the reader to better understand what the music of Buddy MacMaster is all about. He said recently, "I do feel some aches and pain almost everyday. But it seems that whenever I pick up my fiddle and take a few moments to warm up, somehow the pain seems to go away. That's what I feel anyway."

In Tune with Faith

Despite the pain felt through the actions inflicted by some, you may take comfort, a tint of joy and even some personal fulfillment knowing that a person with Buddy MacMaster's qualities and his sense of well-being and caring exists. His music is important, of course. But it is the person first who so many have come to adore and admire. From within that character of calm and quiet emerges a music that is like the person – a rare quality. What are the bases of this gentle man's ways? Obviously, they must rest within his personal convictions and his sense of truth and principles. A devoted Christian, Buddy's unbending respect for his faith is obvious. He attends Sunday Mass regularly, whether at home or on the road touring. He is truly dedicated to its teachings and guidance. The many who know him say his deeds, words and actions convey this dedication.

Upon entering Buddy's home, for example, you can easily see mementoes that reflect his faith and his religion. Among the instruments and other means of making music, visitors can see a small book of prayers, an assortment of religious cards and some complementary wall prints tastefully displayed. None, however, is intrusive to the visitor. Nor are they intended to be. Rather, they are nearby for Buddy to view and use as his time permits. His rosary beads are also nearby, on a table that is situated near a chair where he can sit and relax and privately recite a prayer.

Like the mementoes, Buddy does not impose upon others his religious views or his solemn duties, indeed what he considers are his heartfelt obligations. He seeks a variety of ways to find his own level of satisfaction for, and opportunity to, worship. He appreciates, as well, that people have to find their own way to their own God, their Creator. As people come to know Buddy, they understand that he is tolerant of differing views on a range of subjects. He'll engage in discussions that help clarify and indeed challenge his outlook and thus reaffirm his commitment to his faith and to his music as well. He'll listen carefully and reflect on what is being said or performed to determine how he as an individual might be more understanding and thoughtful or steadfast in his own style of music, whatever the case may be.

Buddy acquired his religious values from his community of Judique, a community with a longstanding tradition with the Roman Catholic faith. The people had arrived from the Old Country with a deep sense of faith. Some, although persecuted, had held steadfast to their beliefs and the early settlers to the Judique area nurtured that commitment to the church. Initially, language among the Scots would be a barrier to celebrating community worship, as the majority of the Scots who had settled the area were all Gaelic speakers. Church worship at that time was under the French-speaking authority of the Quebec Diocese. Later, however, Reverend Alexander MacDonell, a Gaelic-speaking priest, was appointed to Judique in 1818. Subsequently, the community established a church, a glebe and a cemetery, located near the water at Indian Point, culminating eventually in the first parish of Highlanders in Cape Breton – St. Andrew's Parish. The present-day church, the third built in Judique, had its cornerstone laid in 1924 under the new authority of the Antigonish Diocese. Then, in 1927, Archbishop Morrison consecrated the church as St. Andrews, a dedication to the Patron Saint of Scotland.

The church has always been a significant catalyst for building community in Judique. In addition to worship, it also nurtures the social well-being of the parishioners and the extended community. The church makes provisions for the Celtic music and, in particular, the rendering of Gaelic songs through worship and prayer. There are formal and informal organizations, like the parish council, that contribute to fundraising,

Buddy renders pastoral airs with his sister Betty Beaton at St. Joseph's Church, North Sydney, in the early 1990s.

Buddy with Jean Vanier, founder of L'Arche, during a Cape Breton visit.

to building community spirit, and to addressing the needs of the young and the old. St. Andrew's Parish fosters a participatory role for parisoners in religious and lay activities throughout the diocese of Antigonish, and Buddy has consistently taken part in this development.

Buddy nurtures many fine qualities that have been embedded over generations of his people. The people have adapted to a sometimes difficult and harsh environment to cultivate a unique expression of music and dance that after two hundred years of sowing remain true to their Scottish roots. Buddy embodies all the collective good that his home community of Judique in Inverness County has to offer. The old cliché "it takes a village to raise a child" might conjure for Buddy something like "it takes a community to shape a music tradition." Buddy's values have shaped his love for and devotion to his music. He believes his music is a gift that was given to him and is to be shared with family and friends and anyone who has an interest in listening. Buddy says, "The music really belongs to the people."

Buddy's sincere capacity to share, as only he can, deserves recognition. He values the place of music in the community. Yet, as a musician, he performs only where he is invited; he seeks no performance or engagement. He has no agent or manager. This has always been the case. He does not solicit producers or directors to ask whether he might perform amidst the bright lights, the cameras, the fame and the grandeur. To "book" him for a formal engagement, in the professional manner, one simply calls his home. He then checks the calendar that is hanging on the wall and near the telephone. If the date one requests is open, he will "mark" it in the calendar. Sometimes compensation is discussed but just as often it is not. He trusts that if the person who called is kind enough to ask him to play, then that person will be kind enough to make certain he is looked after.

This strong connection with church and community has been, and continues to be, a source of inspiration and motivation for Buddy to share his music worldwide. Buddy MacMaster offers people interested in heritage generally and music in particular an opportunity to better understand the old music tradition from whence he has emerged. Thus, he is a Cape Breton icon.

Today, many people who enjoy the Scottish music say they derive that joy from having experienced the performances of Buddy MacMaster. There is little doubt that the masterful performances by Judique's own "Buddy," as he is affectionately known, conjure up an excitement for the music and the dancing that is often described as "almost infectious." Indeed, for decades, Buddy's music has captured the attention of many people from all walks of life far beyond the shorelines of Cape Breton.

To explore and to understand this worldly phenomenon of Buddy MacMaster and his music, it is important, and in fact necessary, to come to know Buddy the person. For this reason, we will begin a walk with Buddy in Judique, his home. The walk will take into account some of what has already been written and said about Buddy and his beloved Judique.

Judique – Fair is the Place

The community of Judique juts along coastal waters northward from the northern periphery of Creignish near Long Point to the southern boundary of Port Hood near Little Judique and is divided into Judique North and Judique South. Between these two divisions are Hillside, Judique Interval, St. Ninian, River Denys, Rear Long Point and Centennial. Heaven help the person who should say that so-and-so is from Judique South if, in fact, that person hails from Judique North.

This sense of place is important to most people in the communities of Inverness County, Cape Breton, a small body of land nestled along the Atlantic Ocean and situated at the eastern end of the province of Nova Scotia. This sense of place is more pronounced in some communities than in others. For example, located just a short distance from Judique are several communities within a ten-mile radius of Margaree, including Margaree Valley, Margaree Centre, Margaree Harbour, Margaree Forks, North East Margaree and South West Margaree. The exact location of one's birthplace within the Margaree(s) is vital to a Margaree-er's identity. If one was born and raised in Margaree Valley, then to simply say he or she "comes from" Margaree is not sufficient – include the "Valley" or else!

Some claim that the name "Judique" is derived from an Aboriginal word meaning water. Others claim that the name is derived from a French word meaning "a river or stream where the water turns swiftly, forming eddies." One legend has it that Nicholas Denys, an early trader/settler in Cape Breton and Acadia in the mid-seventeenth century, was once passing by Judique in his boat while he read the Book of Judith. While observing the beauty of the area, he wrote in his log the word "Judic," which later gave rise to the name "Judique." Reviewing the Book of Judith, you will find in Chapter 16 the "Hymn of Praise" in which Verse 1 says:

> Strike up the instruments,
> A song to my God with timbrels,
> Chant to the Lord with cymbals;
> Sing to him a new song ...

This verse may have preoccupied Nicholas Denys at the time.

In its early settlement, Judique's excellent coastline, coves and beaches allowed the fishing industry to develop for generations. The area served effectively as a small fishing outlet for the French in particular. Later, farming was deemed as having some potential as a way of life as well.

The early immigrant Scottish settlers who had found their way to the area were determined to build a community. The bard Michael MacDonald (Michael Mor), who came to Judique from Scotland by way of Prince Edward Island, arrived in 1775. He was born on South Uist in 1745 and was Judique's first pioneer. It was during the winter of 1775 that Michael Mor is said to have composed the only one of his songs now extant, *O s alain an-t-ainte* (Fair is the place):

> Fair is the place,
> I have here by the sea,
> When it comes to till it, with the plough.

Sister Margaret MacDonell writes in *The Emigrant Experience*, "The song is of great interest, since it is reasonably certain that it is the oldest extant Gaelic commentary on pioneer life in Cape Breton. If it was composed as early as 1775, that bard must have been contemplating future possibilities rather than the harsh realities of the environment at that time." The harsh realities may have prevailed, but the music flourished in Judique and throughout Inverness County.

A People's Passion

"The highway to happiness is filled with a passion for music," say many who live in any of the typical, rural communities of Inverness County. For many, the place invokes a unique pride and a sense of identity that is manifested particularly in the aural history, the faith, the folklore, and the performing and visual arts especially. Preparing for the book *Making a Difference* to commemorate the coming of the "New Millennium," Frank Macdonald, publisher of *The Inverness Oran*, wrote of the people of Inverness County: "We have been gathering names and information about people from Inverness County who have made special contributions during their lifetime. For some, their contributions have had national and international consequences; for others, their contributions have had more impact directly here at home ... What became evident as we gathered these people together under one metaphorical roof is that Inverness County has had a spiritual, social, political and cultural impact that seems way out of proportion to its population (22,000)."

Macdonald adds, "We have discovered great people and/or moments of greatness on the stage, in the rinks, in rodeo, in boxing and wrestling rings, in literature, in social justice, in the Olympics, in journalism, in Gaelic culture, in business and in art."

The internationally acclaimed singer/performer Frances Black visited Cape Breton in 2005, just prior to concerts scheduled in Holland, Denmark and her native Ireland. In an unprompted, if not a more objective declaration of the county's virtues, Black had this to say about Inverness County: "I couldn't believe how strong the culture and the community spirit is ... The music is everywhere and the dance is mind-blowing ... The culture is probably stronger here than in Ireland ... People are very passionate about what they do ... It's the root of all things Celtic."

It is readily understood that a genuine charm that helps foster that community spirit is the insatiable appetite among the people for the music – an appetite that is sometimes best described by informed participants like Black who "come from away." Within the Cape Breton tradition, various labels are often used when discussing "the music." Such labels include Gaelic, traditional and Celtic. The reference to "the music" is all-inclusive.

To say that the music is a vital thread throughout Inverness County is an understatement and when visiting the county you can come to appreciate that the passion for the music is felt throughout. It is in the home first. It is celebrated at outdoor festivals and concerts at local halls, and schools among the young as well as the old. For some, the music takes on a spiritual dimension and is frequently expressed in the church in its secular fashion as well as in a religious format. It has caught the interest of the recording industry and the media generally, as well as educators and researchers and the imagination of entrepreneurs and other facets of the community that depend on the travelling public to support tourism and small business. It has been the mainstay for traditional family gatherings like the annual Broad Cove Scottish Concert founded in 1957. The music acquired international attention in 1973 when the Glendale community hosted the first Festival of Cape Breton Fiddling. Subsequently, the Cape Breton Fiddlers' Association was founded and enjoyed a twenty-fifth anniversary in 2003; it has a membership of fiddlers that is worldwide.

In recent years, the growth and development of the music in Inverness County has helped justify the construction of a world-class performance venue in Mabou (Strathspey Place) and a Celtic Music Interpretative Centre in Judique. The passion for the music prepares young performers and families to entertain professionally, worldwide – family names like Beaton, Rankin, Cameron, MacMaster, MacDonald, MacEachern and MacIsaac are common wherever quality music is performed. Still at home, it contributes to the renowned Celtic Colours International Festival of Celtic music, which is held throughout Cape Breton each October, attracting visitors and musicians from far and near. Through these developments, in part, the music has helped build relations and partnerships that stretch beyond the county boundaries to places in other parts of Canada, the United States and the United Kingdom.

What precipitates the deep passion for the music in areas like Mabou, Glendale, Troy, Creignish and Judique? For some, there are several explanations – "It's heritage" or "It's tradition," they say. "It's in the genes" or "It's in the blood," others say. Many insist, "It's the Gaelic," understood by some to be the language of the Garden of Eden. In an interview with Mary Anne Ducharme, Frank MacInnis says, "There always have been musical families in Creignish and Judique, and all the little areas around us, people who composed music, played fiddle, step-danced, and were pipers – it's part of the air we breathe." Important, however, is the fact that Cape Breton was once an island and still is, despite the causeway. That sense of isolation has given rise to a unique blend of creativity and imagination that has procreated generations of inventiveness and magic centred on the music, a process that began among the pioneer settlers who have been around and near areas like Judique since the mid-eighteenth century.

Among the more discernable explanations for this intense "blend of creativity and imagination" is the fact that a significant segment of the population has its roots among the Islands and the Highlands of Scotland – they are long and deep despite Frances Black's natural tendency to compare with the Irish tradition. Whenever these Scottish roots are probed as they have been and continue to be by writers, scholars, performers, media and researchers generally, they provide some explanation. What is clear is that for many, the music provides a link with the past, helps endure the here and now, and elicits hope for the future.

Understandably, there is much more in addition to the music that triggers the festive community spirit. It is embedded in the wider community's efforts through public and community education to retain not only the old Gaelic language that still persists among some Scots but also the languages of the Acadians and of the First Nations – the Mi'kmaq. These groups in their respective communities foster encouragement and real support to the visual arts, the literature, the dance and the drama that reflect their unique cultures. Collectively, these efforts shape an identity throughout the county that is as much uplifting and traditional as it is progressive and exhilarating. To address the full spectrum of this rich identity, however, is beyond the scope of this publication – that analysis and historical account is for another time. The feature of this book is "the music" as experienced through the world of one Inverness County person in particular – Hugh Allan (Buddy) MacMaster, one of Cape Breton's "master" fiddler/violinists and arguably *the* master fiddler/violinist.

The Family Circle

Buddy MacMaster was born in Timmins, Ontario, in 1924. His parents, John Duncan and Sarah, and Buddy's older sister, Kathleen, had moved there so John Duncan, a hard-rock miner, could work in the mines. Buddy has four other sisters – Jeannie, Genevieve, Betty Lou and Lorraine – and two brothers, Alex and Jerry, who is deceased, all of whom were born in Inverness County. In 1929, Buddy's parents returned to Inverness County, where his father resumed work at the mines. By this time, Buddy's taste for the music had already developed.

Buddy was reared in the traditional setting both in learning and performing. He would listen to and watch for other fiddlers' approaches to rendering the music very carefully. Periodically, he would ask an older fiddler he admired for some direction. But generally, he would approach learning the instrument by "trial and error." That interest in the music came at an early age and was nurtured by his parents. The home environment was important. John Duncan was a fiddler and Sarah was a noted "jigger" – a form of mouth music. She could render or "jig" a slew of tunes that would keep feet tapping for hours. Buddy learned many of the old Gaelic airs from the way his mother would jig the tunes. She loved the music and the joy she felt for the music was something she shared openly and freely. She enjoyed life to the fullest and was always in support of good sessions of music in the house and into the wee hours of the morning.

Buddy can remember becoming hooked on fiddle music when he was three years old. While still in Timmins, as a young boy, he was quick to recognize that fiddler Angus MacMaster, who lived nearby, was encouraging. Like the MacMasters, Angus later returned to Judique where he and Buddy remained in touch. Now the Judique community would begin to shape Buddy's music and as Angus MacMaster was so well respected among the local fiddlers, this gave Buddy the opportunity to see and hear some of the best at that time. He listened and watched intently and was determined to master the art for himself.

There are several written accounts about the early influences. As Buddy told Frances MacEachen in an interview, "I'd be lying in bed jigging tunes. Then I got two sticks of wood and would be rubbing them together pretending I was playing the fiddle. My grandfather, Alain Iain, was up at the house and he saw me at this, so he whittled the pieces of wood down to resemble a violin and a bow. Somewhere along the way I got away from that. I guess I was getting older, saw it was foolish to be rubbing two sticks together."

Buddy explains in a CBC interview, "I was about eleven, I think, when I started to play ... My father's fiddle was in his trunk and I took it downstairs and I remember it was minus one string ... but I did get to play a tune, 'The Rock Valley Jig,' that day and that encouraged me to keep at it ... Fiddling has been my life since I was a kid. So, it just seems that I have to play a bit most days ... or it's not normal."

Buddy vividly recalls his mission to purchase strings. "I remember ... my mother gave me money and I walked up to D.J. MacDonald's store and bought some strings."

His older sister, Kathleen, remembers him practising all the time with that violin and can also recall her little brother getting very frustrated if he didn't get the tune perfect. Later, Buddy's father purchased a fiddle from Ronald Beaton (Raonull Mairi Bhain) from Port Hood. Buddy remembers, "I guess I had that fiddle for a couple of years. I think I was eighteen when someone sat on it and the fiddle got broken."

Buddy has a tremendous capacity to retain detail pertaining to the music. His recall of tunes and music collections is prodigious. His passion for and interest in his family genealogy, for both sides of the family, are no less impressive. These are common traits among the MacMasters.

Like the Gaels from most parts of Cape Breton, there is always that need to know "from whence we come."

The MacMasters (Buddy's father's people) arrived in Judique in the early 1800s. The MacDonalds (Buddy's mother's people) arrived with the coming of James MacDonald to the Judique Banks in 1798 from Moidart, Scotland. The two Scottish pioneer families participated in efforts at early community development. Buddy acquired his interest in genealogy, as he did with the music, at an early age. The kitchen table conversations among family and special visitors were the source of Buddy's information about his family genealogy. He speaks of three and four generations of family as if they were still "just down" from his home in Judique. In his mind, they are still with him. They are called upon to guide him along life's journey.

"It was the talk around the house quite often," says Buddy. "We discussed that at the kitchen table with family and relatives from around the community. It was the thing to do. I always found that interesting. It's good to be able to pass the information to the younger generation.

"I can go back to two first cousins who came to Creignish – one built that stone house in Creignish about 1802, I believe. It's still there. My descendents [come from] one of those first cousins.

"Duncan MacMaster – son of Duncan [Ruadh], son of Hugh – was my great-grandfather. [His people emigrated from Eigg, Scotland, in the early 1800s.] Big Duncan married Sarah MacIsaac. They lived in Hillsdale – back of Judique. They had a family. My grandfather was one of his sons. That would be Hugh MacMaster. He moved to Wolver [Massachusetts]. Later, he moved back down to Cape Breton and settled at Glencoe Station. We used to go there to make the hay. All that was left there was the vacant farm. That's where my father was born. My grandfather [Hugh] bought a place in Port Hood and he built there. The house is still there. My father [John Duncan] was only a young boy when he moved to Port Hood. His brother 'baby' Charles moved to the U.S. It was Charles who sent down a small violin and said that whoever would learn the instrument could have it.

"My father could play ... nice sweet music, you know. His mother could play. I never heard her play but she would play for dances when she was young. She was a Gillis. Her brothers could play. A lot of the music

Buddy with his sister Kathleen enjoying winter in Timmins (about 1927).

John Duncan MacMaster in uniform during World War I .

Sarah MacMaster at the cannery in Judique in the 1930s.

"It must have been an impossible pedestal but to us, as children, our handsome big brother was a hero who could overcome all obstacles – superman. A strong, loving brother who played the game "Blind Man's Bluff" with the children in the cleared kitchen on a dark winter's evening, like nobody else. A father in many ways, a friend, a protector who would always include us, who drew so many joyous and interesting people into our lives and to our home through his music. We are forever entwined!" (Left to right, 1982: Kathleen Beaton, Betty Beaton, Jerry MacMaster, Lorraine MacDonnell, Buddy, Genevieve Whalen, Alex MacMaster, Jeannie Brennan and their mother, Sarah MacMaster.)

came from my father's mother's side. I know that. There is a strong strain of music from that side of the family."

On his mother's side, Buddy further explains that Sarah was the daughter of Alain Iain MacDonald, who was son of John, son of Donald, son of James. Alain Iain married Catherine Gillis. Buddy is quick to recognize that the music is very much part of the extended family. It is found among his relations, far and wide. Of particular note for Buddy is that his maternal grandmother's sister was a grandmother to Dan R. MacDonald, the great composer/fiddler.

Buddy explains, "Dan R.'s father and my mother were first cousins.

See, my grandmother and Dan R.'s grandmother were daughters of this Gillis lady from Arisaig. She was a grandmother to Alex Francis MacKay, the fiddler, as well. Her mother, a Gillis, was from Arisaig, Antigonish. And she was a cousin to fiddler Wilfred Gillis's father. I am also related to Cape Breton fiddler Winnie Chafe on her mother's side, in two or three ways. Winnie's grandfather, who lived in North Sydney, was a MacDonald and his people came from Judique Banks."

Dan R. MacDonald, Alex Francis MacKay, Wilfred Gillis and Winnie Chafe are all significant links with "the music." They are all of Buddy's generation. There are countless others of both older and younger generations who are related to Buddy and who also have a significant link to the music and the dance. But to identify all would require a publication that might resemble a telephone directory.

Buddy's extended family is large, and kinfolk on all sides of the family are important to him. Donnie "Little Duncan" MacDonald of East Bay tells about his affection for his cousin Buddy and his music. Donnie is related through his father, "Sandy Malcolm's crew." Recording home music sessions since 1954, he has also compiled an extensive personal collection of the music of many Cape Breton fiddlers. Donnie explains, "I have a home recording of Buddy MacMaster that was made in 1945. In my estimation, he will no doubt go down in history as one of Cape Breton's greatest exponents of Scottish music. I consider Buddy to be ranked among the best of Cape Breton Scottish fiddlers."

As a young boy, Donnie would visit his grandfather in River Denys. John Duncan would often visit there, too. "And there was always music. Buddy would sometimes visit and play." Donnie explains that his paternal aunts Margaret, Mabel and Jessie especially adored Buddy and his music. Of the three, two lived and worked in the United States for many years. When Jessie returned to Cape Breton in her older years, Donnie explains humorously, "Buddy would always play for her birthday. He played for her last birthday. She died one week later. She lived to be 107.

"In 1973, I took Aunt Jessie to the Glendale Fiddlers Festival. Archie Neil Chisholm and Rod Chisholm were the Masters of Ceremonies. They introduced a fiddler to take the stage but it wasn't Buddy. It was not yet his turn to perform. Aunt Jessie was getting impatient. She began to yell from her seat, a wooden bench. The concert was outdoors, you understand. It was in Father John Angus's farm field, behind the church. And she wanted Buddy MacMaster to play, you know. We laughed and tried to have her settle down but there was no way she was going to be quiet. She wanted Buddy and that was it. Later, of course Buddy played, to her delight.

"I told Buddy recently that I recall one occasion when I visited my grandfather in River Denys. I was only ten years of age. That evening we took a horse and wagon and made our way to Port Hood to Jessie Gillis's place. She was a cousin of my grandfather. The fiddler that night was Big Alex MacDonald – from the Mabou Coal Mines. Buddy told me that he knew Big Alex's music. Many years ago, he sent me a tape of Big Alex and a tape of John Batherson – the fiddler. That would be [rock/blues performer] Matt Minglewood's grandfather. It's a small world."

And it is. An exciting musical event for the MacMaster family and Cape Breton was the performance by the Grammy Award-winning White Stripes at Glace Bay's Savoy Theatre in July 2007. The person behind the group is Jack White of Detroit. For the Cape Breton concert, a tenth-anniversary special for the band, a thirty-member crew and staff from *Rolling Stone* magazine accompanied the group. It attracted a sell-out international audience. Cape Breton fiddler Ashley MacIsaac opened. In a CBC Radio feature, produced by Jenna MacNeil for *Information Morning*, Buddy describes the MacMaster link with Jack White through generations of Gillis and MacIsaac relations. Buddy explains that through John Gillis, Jack White is a descendent of Duncan MacIsaac, who was a first cousin to Buddy's grandfather – Hugh MacMaster. Buddy proudly declares, "I'd be a third cousin to Duncan MacIsaac's grandson … who would be Jack's father."

While playing at the Red Shoe Pub the next day, Buddy commented, "It was quite a time. They're great musicians. I played a few tunes myself on stage. It was a full house and everyone was enjoying the evening. I didn't get back to Judique until the early morning hours. But I got to church this morning and I made it this afternoon to the Red Shoe. Joey [Beaton] and I have been here for a few hours."

The Farm

By the 1930s, Judique's pioneers had developed a significant scattering of farms. These pioneers would hold fast to their own code of decent living. Respect for family and neighbour and Christian values prevailed, giving clear direction of right and wrong for most. But the people of Judique have known abusive behaviour toward one another too, and that would sometimes manifest itself in cruel ways. Such was the case for a young Buddy MacMaster.

Buddy attended the local school like other kids in his community. Much to his chagrin, some of his classmates often bullied him. He was teased and ridiculed often for his gentle ways. He took offense to this, of course. Buddy's sister Jeannie recalls a school incident when one particular group of boys took matters to the extreme one day. While the teacher was at home for lunch, leaving the students to look after one another, some rallied together, bundled Buddy in his own coat, and then hung him by the coat from a hook at the back of the classroom. His sister Kay pleaded with his classmates to help him down but they refused. "Young Donald Rankin was the only one of the boys who tried to come to Buddy's rescue, but the bullies were determined. They kept Donald away and Buddy remained on that bloody hook until the teacher had returned."

The incident was stressful for young Buddy, Jeannie recalls, but especially for Kay. Jeannie explains, "There were tears in her eyes for what they had done to Buddy. She was very, very upset."

As Buddy was often called upon to defend himself from school bullies who persisted in abusing him, he would learn, in time, to prepare a pretty good line of defense. As a young adolescent, he developed a reputation as someone you wouldn't want to tangle with. As one man said, chuckling, "I heard he was pretty sharp with his fists in his younger days. But I don't know for sure."

Buddy had the usual farm boy's tasks. He loaded the hay wagon. He would tend to the hogs, the hens, and whatever else required attention and sometimes complain about it. Often Buddy's sisters would listen and watch while he milked the cows. When all was calm, the sisters took delight hearing his lilting voice singing to a rhythmic pattern while milking. His favourite lyrics for the milking were those of the "Festival Song." For his sisters, it was often a comical sight and a sound to behold. His sister Jeannie recalls, "He would always look so content just sitting on the bucket, tapping his foot, and singing away. He had a pretty good voice, but he became a much better fiddler, of course." [Jeannie laughs.]

There were other sights and sounds around the barn. Some brought more laughter but a dangerous side, too. Jeannie shared a story about the day Buddy decided to take Tilly, the mare, for a ride – a routine event. Tilly and Buddy had a good relationship as far as Buddy was concerned. On this particular day, Tilly was not in the mood for Buddy, as he would discover. But all did seem fine while he put the bridle on. Buddy then jumped on her bare back and proceeded with a slow trot down the winding, dusty driveway. Jeannie recalls, "The house was so far off the highway, you know. It was okay in the summer, but the winter was not much fun. We all dreaded that long walk." Tilly suddenly took off at a swift gallop along the driveway toward the old storefront perched along the narrow highway. And now there was no stopping her.

Patrons in the store at the time noticed something quickly darting past the front window. Several took to the doorway to see what the commotion was all about. They could recognize Tilly but was that Buddy holding on, they wondered? By this time, Buddy had lifted his upper body toward the back of Tilly's neck and head and was struggling to

The MacMaster family returned to Judique from Timmins, Ontario. Left to right: Kathleen, Buddy and Jerry.

The old homestead in Judique.

Young Buddy MacMaster with one of his first fiddles.

hang on. Now the only part of Buddy's anatomy that the store patrons could see was his bouncing rump. No matter how determined Buddy was to have Tilly slow down and make her way back toward the barn, this was not going to happen until Tilly was good and ready. Eventually, she stopped galloping, slowly turned around, and began to make her way back toward home with Buddy continuing to grasp her mane – for dear life. Upon reaching the barn, Buddy slithered off Tilly and when he felt secure with his two feet firmly on the ground, he looked at Tilly and shouted, "You Goddamn bastard." Rather out of character for Buddy, many would agree.

Horses were an integral part of the daily scene around the MacMaster farm. Buddy's father, John Duncan, was well-known for breeding horses. He recognized the dangers inherent in the work and had always taught his family to be careful around the horses and to treat the animals with respect. In the horse business, however, dangers are always lurking and despite all the caution, trouble is by no means remote.

On one occasion, John Duncan was holding the reins for one of the more frisky horses. The horse was jumpy and John Duncan proceeded to try and calm the horse down. Nearby was a young mare that began to make its way toward the horse, which became more excited and made several attempts to free itself from John Duncan, as if to reach out for the approaching young mare. Seeing this, John Duncan pulled on the reins to lead the horse toward the barn and then inside. The horse appeared to settle down but only momentarily. Suddenly, the horse turned its head abruptly toward John Duncan and proceeded to sink its huge teeth into John Duncan's left wrist. It was as though the horse wanted to punish John Duncan for being kept from the mare.

The bite was severe and John Duncan realized that he was in trouble, but he was determined to settle the horse in his stall. The horse prepared for a second attack. This time it pinned John Duncan against the barn wall, spreading its hind legs and steadying itself so as to maximize its power and strength with full force against John Duncan, who remained pinned until he fell to the barn floor. The dust from the feed and the dry hay had already filled the stall area and John Duncan was now gasping for air. Eventually, he managed to crawl away and free himself from further danger.

Back at the house, later that evening, the local doctor carefully examined the bite, diagnosed its condition and decided that the arm must be removed at a point near the left shoulder. It was expected that the poison from the bite would spread quickly. A huge swelling had already taken hold by this time. Sarah, however, would have none of this as a solution. She dismissed everyone around her so that she might take charge and fix this situation. Her private vigil began. Daily she washed the wound with a series of homemade remedy treatments. Subsequently, the injury healed and John Duncan's use of the wrist and the full arm was restored.

"The frisky horse was not yet finished," Buddy explains. "He attacked again not long after that. And the darn bugger managed to get yet another slight bite. The victim this time was myself. I can chuckle now [and he does] but at the time it was darn scary. He got me in my left hand. There was no serious damage, however. I got over it. And my father recovered, too. He and the horse were pretty tough." [Buddy laughs.]

The Farm Fades

The sights and sounds of young Buddy's Judique were much different than today. The whistle of the *Judique Flyer* making its way along the train tracks with passengers and freight and the screaming cries of the gulls announcing the return of the fishing boats would generate excitement among the residents. Meanwhile, the farmers were gearing up for a good day's work. Depending on the season, you could hear the workings of new machinery and see new barns being built, the haymaking gear in full motion, and the planting or harvesting of crops. Dairy cattle leaving the barns would cross the gravel road, making their way to pasture and back again. The sheep were not far behind. The lambs, much to their chagrin, were herded toward the tracks and like the pulp from the local sawmill were readied for export to distant places. Community historian Jim St. Clair of Mull River describes this early Judique as one of "vibrancy of growth and tradition."

The Gaelic language was the language of choice among the early pioneers for socializing as well as for business and commerce. St. Clair describes the area residents' interest in the old Highland traditions: "Well, in Gaelic conversation, people would reveal how their memories extend back to the coming of immigrants from the Islands and Highlands of

Scotland ... Their descendents could still recall the dangers of travel in small sailing ships crossing the North Atlantic ... and then the heavy work of clearing land and building houses and barns."

Buddy's recollection of these stories and the importance of the Gaelic language are vivid, too. In his account of that era, he says, "I think that in those years the neighbours were more neighbourly, so to speak. There was more visiting, and there was more entertainment in the home among the neighbours. There'd be music and playing cards or telling stories. That's a kind of lost art, to tell stories. A lot of the older people spoke in Gaelic. They seemed to enjoy the stories much more in Gaelic than in English."

In the late 1930s, the local residents and those from the neighbouring countryside would make their way among the few small stores available in the Judique community. Jackie MacDougall, first cousin to both Buddy and his wife Marie, explains that several stores emerged over the years that had a special place in the community. "There was one down here at Judique Interval ... they called it the canteen ... McKillop had that one and then my father had a store here and then there was the cooperative store ... That's where Smith's store was ... MacInnis has it now ... and then up where the fire hall was a big, big store. They had a dry goods store and in the basement they had the liquor store ... And then a little further south they had a grocery ... whatever you could think of was in that – it was really ahead of its time, at the time – when [Port] Hawkesbury had a big supermarket that did away with the local stores."

Long before Port Hawkesbury's appeal, store patrons arrived in horse and buggy and were accustomed to stocking essential supplies for the long winters and the labour-intensive summers. Exchanging produce like butter and eggs and new potatoes for imported merchandise like kerosene and sugar was commonplace. As a young boy, Buddy sometimes worked in the general store owned by Jackie MacDougall's father.

Buddy explains to Burt Feintuch, "They also sold workboots and dress shoes. Molasses came in 45-gallon puncheons or 90-gallon puncheons, I think – big wooden puncheons of molasses and kerosene. That's before we got electricity. Sweet biscuits and cookies came in bulk in a box. Oatmeal came in a big bag – I don't know how many pounds would be in it. It would be like the old 98-pound bags of flour. I used to work in the store sometimes, the little store down here. I sure remember pumping a

49

lot of gallons of molasses and filling up jugs with kerosene down there ... They sold beef. The merchant would buy the beef or exchange it for groceries. It was a different ball game altogether."

On one occasion, Buddy's limited Gaelic language skills were put to the test. Jackie MacDougall recalls, "My father used to get Buddy to come to the store if he had to go away, you know. This day, I was only a little fellow – six or seven – Buddy was looking after the store and this old fellow came in ... He was upset over something ... I don't know what it was ... he was pretty cross ... and he stood back and he gave Buddy the darnest blast ... The guy had no mercy whatsoever but he couldn't speak English; it was all in Gaelic ... and Buddy couldn't understand what he was saying anyway ... and Buddy was behind the counter and every once in awhile Buddy would say, '*Tha* [yes], *Tha* [yes]' ... Eventually, the old fellow left. He did not know that Buddy could not speak the Gaelic."

In time, the homestead and farm had all but disappeared from the MacMaster family's responsibilities. So that the farm would not be abandoned completely and to help keep some music around the old place, Buddy decided to organize a series of what became famous dances in the old barn. Buddy remembers, "We decided to start a camping ground and the old barn, which was a big barn – seventy-five or so feet long – we converted that to a dance hall ... put in a hardwood floor. So, we ran dances there and they came from all over – Sydney to New Glasgow. I guess it was something new to be in a barn ... lots of parking space. We got Estwood Davidson, quite a good guitar player [and] one of my sisters playing piano."

That adventure came to a sudden stop after only a brief period, however, when the barn was destroyed by fire.

But there were other developments outside the early farm lifestyle that would have an even greater impact on Buddy. Formal education in the Judique community had emerged in the late nineteenth century. Janette MacDonald, in her undergraduate essay, provides some interesting background on the community development of Judique. A high school opened in 1945 and marked the opening of the first consolidated school in the province of Nova Scotia. At the time, the nine one-room schools in the Judique area were closed. Other developments emerged, too. In 1933, for example, the United Maritime Fisherman's Union built the cannery. The Co-op opened in 1936. With these developments, transportation improved.

In 1955, the Canso Causeway was constructed, allowing for a more direct link between Cape Breton and mainland Nova Scotia. Travel to Judique was now along Highway 19, later named the "The Ceilidh Trail." The journey is promoted as a must for visitors and tourists to the area. A Province of Nova Scotia tourist guide says, "The Ceilidh Trail offers stunning vistas of rugged coastline, bays and inlets, verdant hills and rolling farmlands as it follows the shore of western Cape Breton ... from the causeway to the Cabot Trail ... From Port Hastings to Judique, the Ceilidh Trail traces the rugged beautiful coastal plain that lies between St. George's Bay and the thickly wooded Creignish Mountain. Along the way the Ceilidh Trail passes through the picturesque village of Creignish ... the beauty of these hills, and their similarity to parts of the Scottish Highlands, made this region particularly attractive to the Scottish settlers of the late 1700s and early 1800s."

David Stephens, who researched a history of railroads in Nova Scotia, describes the Canadian National Railway's (CN) efforts to build an eastern Nova Scotia link which began with the formation of the Abbott-Allan group in Halifax in 1876 and the construction of the Truro to Cape Breton railway. Following some financial difficulties, the Nova Scotia government took over the company in 1883. By 1891, the line between the Strait of Canso and Sydney was completed, passing along the Bras d'Or Lakes and through Iona. The line between the Strait of Canso and St. Peter's had been built earlier. The proposed St. Peter's to Louisbourg link never materialized. By the 1890s, a small railway operated in Inverness under the direction of W.P. Hussey but it was not until 1901 that the Inverness line (the Inverness Railway and Coal Company) was connected to Point Tupper with the sole purpose of hauling coal from the mines at Inverness, Mabou and Port Hood.

Buddy beginning his CN career, 1943.

Buddy MacMaster began work with CN in 1943. He explains his early interest in acquiring work at CN. "I used to be around the tracks and around the station. I was just a young boy. It looked like a pretty good job. Everyone else was working in the woods or fishing. The agent said something to me once. I guess that was in my mind.

"One day I was at the Co-op store up here. The store clerk gave me a telegram and asked me to take it down to the station. I was coming down anyway. I went to the station ... I was seventeen years old then. I told McCormack [the station agent] I was interested in getting into the station and to learn the station work – the telegraphy. He gave me a New Glasgow address to write the superintendent. I got word back that the agent [in Judique] would take me. They were hungry for operators then. They were short of men – it was the war years. Meanwhile, I was working along the roads at the time to earn money. You had to earn some money, too, and help out.

"Then the month of May came along and the agent said [I] may as well go up and write the rules [the exam]. He called New Glasgow and talked with the chief train dispatcher ... Anyway, I go up to New Glasgow and I was staying at a hotel next to the station. The dispatcher's office was upstairs. I went up to see the chief ... I wrote the rules and got along fine and then I had to have my telegraphy test ... I got along great. I went back to see the chief and he had the reports of the test.

"He said he would be glad to have me come to work ... They'd likely have me work on another station on the mainline to practise with the train orders. This all came pretty suddenly, you know. You can begin work tomorrow, he said. [Buddy gives a hearty laugh.]

"I came down [to Judique] on the train [to get things ready for work]. The next day I pulled out at 8:25 in the morning. I went to Point Tupper [by train] and got on the Sydney to Halifax train. Then they got that train on the train ferry and crossed to Mulgrave. It would take the train all day to get to Truro. So it was 4:30 when I got to the Valley Station [near Truro] and I was to go to work at six o'clock ... that was May 14, 1943."

As part of his work at CN, Buddy would take instructions over the telegraph key. The instructions were prepared as typed material on paper and readied for distribution among the crews of passing trains.

He says, "There were a lot of trains. You know 'meeting' trains and passing up orders – 'wide orders,' they called them. Caution [at night] was a yellow signal and in the daytime, the signal was straight up [an arm] and that was to proceed; half down was when you had orders for the train."

Between 1943 and 1949, Buddy's work at CN was steady but at different train stations in Cape Breton and mainland Nova Scotia. As he became a more experienced operator in his career as a railway worker, he would often find himself on a construction train fixed in one location and not in close proximity to a station yet still having to forward and receive instructions and update information. He would climb a nearby telephone pole and attach a device to the wires for communicating with the dispatcher using a radiophone. In the industry's lingo, he was making a drop.

At one point early in his career with CN, he had acquired a permanent position in Judique but due to the 1947 mine strike, there was less need for operators. He was displaced for having little seniority. "They didn't need the night operators so they cut out those jobs. Some guys had more seniority than I had so I got displaced in Judique and I had to go out displacing. If somebody reported sick ... the younger fellows who did not have seniority to get a permanent job travelled around to the different stations."

Before arriving at the Antigonish station in 1948, Buddy was in North Sydney for a year. He had now become accustomed to shift work, taking the two-to-ten or four-to-midnight shift and sometimes the midnight-to-eight a.m. slot. As the Antigonish station would see plenty of passenger trains, Buddy would often be required to work some early evenings.

In 1949, Buddy was appointed station agent in Mabou, a managerial position. Things were to be a bit more settled for the twenty-four-year-old Buddy now. He would board at the MacMillan home in Mabou. The Mabou arrival is a turning point in some ways. He would fare better in terms of money and there was a sense of permanency for him. Later, we shall see that his music would begin to come into its own. The station, however, was busy. There were people and supplies "coming and going" and Buddy had responsibility to keep the work site in order. He recalls he issued passenger tickets, looked after the books and assumed responsibility for the freight trains. In fact, he would assume significant responsibility at all future stations where he worked from that point.

He was in the Mabou station for five years (1949–1954) before returning to the Judique station, where he remained for nine years. By now, downsizing was underway. But the work was as busy as ever. He was back on the "spare board" once again and on the move among the local stations. During this time, there was no shortage of places at which Buddy could board.

One place in particular where he left a lasting impression was at the home of Linden MacIntyre's parents in Port Hastings. Linden MacIntyre of CBC's *Fifth Estate* recalls, "I've known him and his music for nearly sixty years ... since a charmed winter when he was a boarder for a period in my parents' home in Cape Breton. Later, in my teens, I was a frequent guest in his parents' home ... His music and the music of people inspired by him became an internal sound track in my consciousness, a crucial reminder of who I am and where I come from ... no matter where I go."

By early 1964, he got work at the Port Hawkesbury station briefly before moving on to Avondale. As an agent, Buddy explains, "I was there a few months that winter. Avondale was a busy train order office. At one time, Avondale was one of the busiest [stations]." Shortly thereafter, he was back to Port Hawkesbury where he assumed responsibility for the gypsum train. Again, he would travel on the train to River Denys. Buddy recalls, "To check the tonnage ... I'd go down for noon and go back to Point Tupper in the evening. The routine would be repeated later and that would give good overtime. I was four years on the gypsum train. I left that and went to St. Peter's. The agent retired there ... You could hold a permanent job and bid on a temporary job and still hold the permanent one. Some of these stations were up for closure and they were advertising for temporary jobs only."

Over the next several years, Buddy moved from station to station, remaining at Mabou for an extended time before concluding his CN career in 1988 after fourteen years with the Havre Boucher station.

John Howarth, from Prince George, British Columbia, has a passion for Canadian train heritage. He began work for the railway in 1969 where he started out as a brakeman mostly with construction trains. He is now retired from conventional railroading activities and instructs at the British Columbia Institute of Technology (BCIT), where he teaches people how to drive trains and currently instructs in the conductor's training program. John's interest in trains and in music resulted in an opportunity to meet and to fully appreciate one of his idols – Buddy MacMaster.

"For the last ten or fifteen years, I've had a strong interest in Celtic music and that kind of music goes hand in hand with the name of Buddy MacMaster ... CBC Radio has played his music and we have nationwide programming that allows you to hear stuff from other parts of the country. So, whenever I heard Buddy was coming on, I would stop and pay attention ... then realizing that he had not been a [professional/full-time] musician all his life, that he actually had a railway career for many years, was even more interesting ... He is certainly like a folk icon of Canadian culture.

"I went to see him at one of the venues in Cape Breton at the Celtic

Colours Music Festival 2005 ... Before the show actually got started, my friend Marlene [MacInnes] introduced me to him; she knows him ... so that was kind of my first and only meeting with Buddy MacMaster ... It was a privilege to meet him. And I sat down and talked to him briefly about railroading and he was more than happy to share. He's such a regular guy."

In 1999, John helped produce a program with CBC Radio called *The Rupert Rocket* (the local name for the train *The Skeena*, that VIA Rail operates between Jasper, Alberta and Prince Rupert, British Columbia). The idea was to bring local musicians on board between Jasper and Prince George. The two-hour radio broadcast featured the musicians' performances and interviews with some of the local travellers on the train.

"I have Buddy's recording of *The Judique Flyer* ... named after the old steam-driven passenger train ... Like the *Rupert Rocket*, it has its own folklore and stories. I understand that it replaced the old stagecoach line running between Inverness and Point Tupper. I'm told that Buddy often travelled the *Judique Flyer* train as a young boy and played many tunes on his fiddle during those travels ... Legend has it that he travelled it to come home from his first away-from-home dance in nearby Port Hastings."

Buddy relates a story about playing his fiddle on the local trains. "Well, I'd sometimes play a few tunes to pass the time away. Most people did not seem to mind. Some looked like they enjoyed it. I remember this one time, I was travelling on a train and I felt like playing a tune. I don't know where I was ... somewhere on the mainland. Anyway, this woman was sitting across from me. She looked kind of cross. I was not sure if I should play the fiddle or not. But I decided I would give it a try. I played for a bit and then I could see her foot tapping to the music. So I thought ... well ... she is okay. I think she was enjoying it too ... but she continued to look cross just the same."

Buddy may have played a few tunes while travelling on the *Judique Flyer* and on other trains in Nova Scotia and especially in Cape Breton, but he also played a few tunes while at work for CN. In a CBC interview on the occasion of Buddy's eightieth birthday, Jim Nunn asked how he got to play the fiddle on the dedicated lines. Buddy replied, "[On] lots of nights ... as it was getting near time for me to go off duty and it would be quiet as the trains would have run ... the dispatcher would say, 'Now get out your five-dollar fiddle and give us a tune.' So, that's what I would do ... I was in pretty good with them all, you know."

John Howarth explains, "Dedicated lines carried communication between the train dispatcher and the operator, much in the way that an intranet would work. The telegraph poles would usually have a number of sets of wires, some of which were used for other purposes like public telegraphs or maintenance forces, but there were always dedicated lines for use by the dispatchers and operators to issue instructions for the movement of trains. In today's world those communications are transmitted by radio often with repeater towers or satellite links. The dedicated lines were intended only for train movement business and would have been audited to make certain this was complied with. That Buddy was able to use them to share his music speaks to the less formal procedures in Cape Breton."

In conversation with John Howarth, the fellow-trainman, Buddy was a bit clearer as to how the music was actually played over the dedicated lines. John shares the following account of how this would work. "In Cape Breton in the different stations he worked in, [Buddy] probably would have had a bit of time on his hands. Some people would say it's a boring job because you're not busy all the time. But Buddy was telling me about having his fiddle at work and how he would have a foot pedal and when they push it down, they can talk to any other operator that's on line. And so sometimes, he would just play his fiddle and he would push the foot pedal and many of the operators that were listening could hear his music. He is quite amazing."

Danny Graham is from Judique. Danny's father Alex worked with Buddy at CN. Alex, a noted step dancer, often exchanged visits with Buddy. Danny says, "They shared a few tunes and a few steps after hours at the CN station in Judique. On Friday evenings when work was done, they went inside [the station] and had a little Kyleakin. If the weather was nice, Buddy would sometime take the fiddle out and he might have some extra visitors along with the workers – have some tunes and some step-dancing and some stories and fun."

Buddy's CN career concluded in 1988 after forty-five years of service. Passenger rail service for all of Cape Breton Island came to a close on January 14, 1990. As Jim St. Clair reminisces, "I watched the lights of the last rail-liner glide into the swirl of snow down the track towards Alba and into oblivion. 'Will ye no come back again?' echoed through my head. But no answer came from the disappearing train."

The Ring

Perhaps it was the daily routine of the *Judique Flyer* coming and going and all that a young boy's imagination could conjure from the romance often attributed to train travel that helped Buddy think about what the rest of the world might have to offer. In any event, the sport of boxing certainly became important to him. His thoughts, indeed his passion, for the sport may have been influenced, too, by the rugged battles with the farm horses or the schoolyard bullies.

Respect for neighbours was a strong feature of life in early Judique, but so was the need to find a way to settle a score fairly and with honour. The ring was one option. According to *Making A Difference*, the community of Judique had already been noted for great achievements in the ring from the heroic deeds of wrestling champion "Judique Dan" MacDonald, who fought 945 bouts in his career. Judique Dan won his greatest triumph when he defeated Sam Anderson of Sweden to earn the Lord Lonsdale Belt, emblem of the World Middleweight Championship. Buddy's acquaintance with Judique Dan might also have contributed to his interest in boxing, which Buddy describes as generational: "The old people were kind of interested in that [boxing]. And if you couldn't fight you weren't much good – years ago, you know ... our grandparents and back even earlier with the ones who came from Scotland ... it was kind of in them, you know."

Buddy's view on this tradition among the Highlanders in the Old Country would find favour with Derick S. Thomson, who writes in *The Companion to Gaelic Scotland*, "Highland pride in clan and race can be seen as a mixed blessing. Mixed with a volatile temperament, it can be the starting point for a bloody feud, yet family pride and a belief that one is related to the head of the family calls for standards of behavior that will not let the side down. While there were fierce quarrels and resulting feuds, Highlanders were noted for being fair and honest in business and for their strong tradition of hospitality to the stranger."

Buddy's reference to the more recent generation of Highlanders relates to a local form of sport without rules and regulations focused on fisticuffs of a rowdy nature that prevailed outside a ring. They were often staged outside a local dance hall and, just as often, inside the hall. "I saw a few of those in my day, too," Buddy chuckles.

His early interest in boxing was nurtured through his association with Walter Gillis, a close relation on his father's side who knew something about the inside of a boxing ring. Walter had lived in the United States for many years and had developed as an amateur boxer. Buddy describes him as "not being bad at all ... based on the accounts I have heard over the years." Walter lived with the MacMasters when he returned to Cape Breton. "He was in his sixties then." Buddy recalls that Gillis saw his stay at John Duncan and Sarah's as an opportunity to teach the young Mac-Master boys some of the skill in boxing. Thus began Buddy's real devotion to the sport.

"Walter Gillis took me aside and showed me how to use my fists, how to jab, and how to hold my arms in position. He explained to me not to move the head too far to the left or too far to the right. You had to move just so. You had to maintain a balance and be prepared to throw a few punches, too. [Buddy is going through the motions in meticulous detail as he explains the "art" of boxing according to Walter Gillis.]

"I bought a pair of boxing gloves in Sydney when I was a kid. I saved my money. I use to box my brother Jerry. Just for fun, of course. We would box out in the backyard, and in the barn, and even in the house. My father got a big kick out of the racket. He used to pretend to be reading the newspaper but he would look over the pages every now and then to get a little glimpse.

"I remember Mother watching when Jerry and I were doing the rounds in the kitchen. Mother was there with the old kitchen clock and keeping time ... The clock would ring and she would separate us until it was time for the next round."

One of the first major fights Buddy recalls was the famous Joe Louis-Art Schmeling championship fight in 1938. Louis's victory was the start of his illustrious boxing career. Buddy recalls, "That fight lasted only thirty-nine seconds. Several of us had gathered in an old car that someone visiting had. Before you know it, it was all over. [Buddy laughs.] I enjoyed Joe Louis and followed most of his fights on radio. Later, I was able to enjoy the old reruns of his fights on TV. I followed the fights of Rocky Marciano and several other great boxers in the '40s and the '50s.

"I remember the Tony Galento-Joe Louis fight in June 1939. [Galento] was an American. He was kind of a fleshy guy. He was a brawler style fighter. He had Louis down on his rear end, you know. That surprised everyone. And then Louis got up and he went to town on him. Louis knocked him out in the fourth round," Buddy concludes, laughing.

One official account of that fight validates Buddy's recollection. The article "Tony Galento" reads, "The fourth round was brutal for Galento, who really had no defense and was wide open for Louis's assault. Louis hit him with murderous combinations, which forced the referee to finally stop the fight."

Buddy kept a close eye on the local scene as well. He would travel to Sydney and to Halifax to catch a fight. He took an interest in the careers of Yvonne Durelle and George "Rock-A-Bye" Ross. He could discuss the various weight differentials of each in meticulous detail. "Yvonne was a powerful guy. I'd say Rock-A-Bye Ross was around 154," Buddy explains.

On one occasion while travelling by plane to perform, Buddy had an opportunity to meet Blair Richardson, a celebrated local boxer and former Middleweight Champion of both Canada and the British Commonwealth, who was travelling on the same plane. "I said hello to him. I recall he was a very gentle person. He was very friendly. I enjoyed watching Tyrone Gardner [a former Canadian Lightweight Champion]. I met him at Rock-A-Bye Ross's funeral, and he recognized me. I was surprised he knew me. Maybe he has a little interest in the music, too.

"I attended the fights whenever I got the chance. I watched some of the important fights in the local hall whenever they patch up to cable. I really enjoyed the [Evander] Holyfield and [Lennox] Lewis fights [in 1999]. Lewis won on both accounts, in my opinion. Lewis is a good fighter. He is a big man. He has a tremendous reach ... I still subscribe to *The Ring* [the popular magazine about boxing]."

Although Buddy's relative Duncan Gillis (1881-1963) from Southwest Mabou was inducted into the British Columbia Sports Hall of Fame in 1967 for his achievements in track and field and wrestling, Buddy turns off any questions about his own aspirations for professional sports with typical gentle humour. He says, laughing, "Well, you know, I don't think I had any notion to do that, but I was kind of part of a professional sport team at one time. I played the national anthem at a baseball game between the Boston Red Sox and the Detroit Tigers. That was June 27, 1997. Perhaps that Cape Breton music helped them to win the World Series a few years later." [He laughs again.]

Spirits of the Time

Indulgence in a wee dram was an aspect of the culture that surrounded the life and times of the Cape Breton fiddler. There were many contributing factors to this trait. The sense of isolation and the challenges of rural living often contributed to and help explain, in part, the sometimes excessive indulgence. There are countless stories one could include in any account of a local fiddler and the effect of the drink. Some are funny, others not so. Nevertheless, it is fair to assume that the drinking habits among the local musicians and the fiddler, in particular, were of concern to many.

For some, alcohol was a way of life and contributed to hardships in family and community. In an earlier generation, some held the view that the fiddle was the instrument of the devil. So much so that in the early 1900s, a member of the clergy actually made his way through Mabou to confiscate the fiddles. It would appear that he really did not succeed in banishing the instrument. One cleric, who today encourages fiddle performance at his weekly Mass, explains that the fiddlers of the parish were clever. "They had two fiddles. They only gave one to the priest and the worst of the two at that. They hid the second beneath the bed."

In the 1950s and the 1960s when the music was enjoying abundance in the homes and in the community, alcohol was present, too, and as Buddy states, "Some bad habits evolved." It was understood that the drink would prevail where the fiddlers were expected to perform at local events like weddings, showers and concerts. It was difficult for the fiddlers to say no to these invitations. Many felt compelled to attend, and Buddy was no exception. In fact, he was called upon frequently because of his popularity as a dance fiddler: "I played for weddings often. I play today for the grandchildren of couples I played for in the '40s. That would represent three generations."

It is common knowledge that some couples planning their weddings would consult with Buddy first to see whether he was available to play for the traditional wedding dance that would take place in the local hall.

"Yes ... I'd get calls to make a booking for a wedding. I always got a kick out of that. Because sometimes they would give a date and I'd say, well, I'm booked that day. There would be a little pause and I could hear some talking in the back[ground] and they would come back and ask if another date was open. It was really funny to hear that. But I guess they felt that the music was important. Sometimes these people were booking a year in advance. I guess that made sense so other stuff had not been booked yet and so there was room to change certain things." [He laughs.]

He did not avoid playing at local events. He felt they were an effective way to practise and to introduce new tunes. And he understood there would be no remuneration but he also understood the temptations to drink would be plentiful and that he would want to partake "just like the next fellow." This, after all, was perceived as a form of payment for the fiddler. The host understood that this was "the proper thing" to do – supply the drink. The idea of a free drink for everyone with an extra supply for the fiddler was the norm. This is simply the way it was. In Buddy's case, he found that his hectic playing schedule would have him consuming alcohol more than he would like and he will admit to having some moments in the past that he would have preferred not to happen.

Buddy explains the temptation around alcohol: "They [hosts] were more generous to the fiddlers. The habits are different today. Thank God. It was as though you took it when it was offered because you might not see it for awhile. [In those days], you could get it in [Port] Hawkesbury if you had a car but that was it. So, when it was made available you took advantage of it. It was even in the car and without fear of the law. The law in the '50s and '60s simply closed an eye to the practice, it would seem."

Buddy's sisters were most understanding and always forgiving. Kay explains, "We used to get so cross when he was having a few. But we couldn't stay cross. He was never out of sorts with us. And no matter what he was doing, his prayers were important to him. He always said his prayers. If he came home late you could hear him saying his prayers before he went to bed.

"I recall one night when whomever he was with hit a deer along the road. Buddy felt so bad for the deer. You could hear him saying out loud from his room how badly he felt for the deer and asked God to forgive him.

"But he was so good to us. He was the big brother and at times he was like a father. He was always there to help. He would make certain we got to school and if there were things we needed he would get it for us. Those of us who played the piano would often be with him at dances and the like. And if he decided to have a few there we would get cross there, too ...

"We'd all take turns making certain that his shirts were washed and pressed. It seemed like we were pressing shirts all week for Buddy. I recall the shirts were all lined up for him. He needed so many for his dances, especially in the summer. For one dance he would need at least two and sometime three shirts. And he always wanted a white shirt – crisp white. That was and still is important to Buddy."

The following adventure is in Buddy's own words. "Well, I made my way to the Sydney area this time to play for a dance – it was in the mid-1960s, I recall. I believe I was working on the mainland then. I was a little late getting there because of the distance. A.J. Campbell was with me. I played for a bunch of sets that night. It was a good dance, of course. I know we should have come right back to Judique after the dance but we decided to go into Sydney for a little party. Well, there was plenty to drink, you know. I was having a few. I recall someone had some home-made stuff. Anyway, there was music and no one seemed in a hurry to go home. I know we should have gone at least from there to Judique directly, but again, we didn't. We headed back to where the dance had been the night before and made a visit to a house there. [Buddy laughs.]

"We arrived there in time for breakfast. A.J. was driving and he wasn't drinking so I was in good hands. We had a breakfast and a few tunes and then made our way back to Judique. It was a great time. Those were the good old days! I think it was not so long after that when I decided to change a few bad habits."

Buddy explains that drinking often took place outside the dance halls, in the back of concert stages, in picnic fields and at the home sessions. This was a common practice. Buddy was concerned and responsible enough, however, that he would always want to have another person drive his car, especially if he had a distance to go. He had several gentlemen in the community who he could call upon. In the early days, his good friend A.J. Campbell of Glencoe would do the honours. Later, Joe "Tac" MacDougall from Port Hawkesbury would drive and actually did double duty as the prompter for the sets. So safeguards were taken.

Buddy sums it all up this way: "I was on the wrong track for awhile. But I got over that." [He laughs.]

Archie Neil Chisholm (1907-1997) was a fiddler and wonderful story-teller and came from a community where the music was appreciated and celebrated. He was revered among the local fiddlers, especially, for his display of courage in life. Afflicted with polio as a young boy, he struggled to put himself through school and university and, in later life, conquered his fight with alcohol. His story is eloquently told in Mary Anne Ducharme's book, *Archie Neil: A Triumph of a Life!* He understood the importance of the role model.

In a CBC interview, Archie Neil said, "The younger people began to realize the respect with which the fiddlers now have ... In addition to their natural inclination for music ... they would want to have some of that respect ... and some of that boasting that went with the musicians ... and they began to follow it until we have an army of musicians today ... They say that imitation is the most sincere form of flattery ... There are a dozen players, among the young ones today, who would try to imitate

Buddy ... in the fact that they want to be miniature Buddys. That has led them to struggle and fight to be as good as he is and this has done a tremendous amount for music."

Buddy was determined that alcohol would not get the best of him. He succeeded even before he had settled down to married life, and for that he acquired a sincere respect from family and friends for his courageous fight.

To receive money in the '50s and the '60s in lieu of a dram would happen only on rare occasions. It fact, when it did happen it would elicit a degree of curiosity, certainly among musicians. As a young fiddler in that era, Buddy may have gotten a little taste of the drink but he also got an early taste of getting paid a little money for his music.

"I got my first real money, if you can call it that, when I was fifteen, I guess. I was asked to play for a dance at the Troy School. It was just a little dance, you know. Anyway, they gave me four dollars. I had to pay my way on the old bus to the dance and then on the train to get home the next day. I remember meeting Dan R. on the train. I told him what I got paid for the dance. He looked at me for a moment and then he said, 'You did well.'"

The money for the dance in Troy in 1939 may have been a small amount but it would symbolize bigger things to come. Buddy had now begun his journey to becoming one of the most popular dance players in Inverness County. The dance circuit would carve out for Buddy a niche that would lead him and his music to new ventures. Eventually, he would need more than the *Judique Flyer* to reach these destinations.

King of the Jig

To talk with Buddy MacMaster about his interest in, indeed his passion for, the music, you will invariably discuss his dance music. It would be extremely difficult to estimate the total number of dances at which he has performed over the years. Some think it to be in the thousands. What is indisputable is that Buddy and his music are inseparable from the uniqueness of Cape Breton dance. Dance Nova Scotia's publication, *No Less No More Just Four on the Floor,* explains, "The incorporation of step dance into the square sets has given Cape Breton a distinct indigenous dance style, with certain configurations specific to particular communities. In terms of cultural richness dancing in Cape Breton is a gold mine! ... Today the main stronghold of Cape Breton dance is Inverness County, where both the Scottish Sets and the Cheticamp Acadian Sets have enjoyed uninterrupted popularity."

When the square dance scene arrived in Inverness County is not totally clear. Following her review of published material and interviews, Emily Addison writes in her 2001 dissertation, "My general understanding in terms of the beginning of the halls was that prior to 1900 ... picnics, weddings, and the home were where dancing occurred. Schoolhouses began to host dances in the early 1900s ... Community, private or public dance halls came into existence in the late 1930s or 1940s."

The early dance hall setting was very crude. There were no sound systems until the 1950s. One way fiddlers would try and compensate for the poor acoustics was to join with a second fiddler, and in those days Buddy would often team up with Hughie T. MacDonell. One technique they often used was to have one fiddler "play on the back strings" while the second played "the high strings." This would give more volume to the music and allow the dancers to have a greater chance to hear the music more clearly.

Buddy began a regular dance circuit as early as 1949. He was then at the CN train station at Mabou. By this time, Buddy had developed as a great dance player – timing, repertoire, stamina, availability – and he felt a sense of personal satisfaction performing for dancers. This was his stated objective as a young musician – to be a good dance player. Now he was beginning to be recognized as such.

Before Mabou, however, he had little opportunity to play for dances. He worked mostly on the mainland, doing the four to twelve shift, and the square dance scene on the mainland was not as prevalent as in Cape Breton. He did make occasional visits to Halifax where the resident Cape Breton population were interested in "down-home" dances. Winston "Scotty" Fitzgerald (1914-1987) was into the Halifax scene at that time as well. Winston had established himself as one of Cape Breton's most popular fiddlers of his day, through commercial recordings, radio and television appearances, and an extensive dance circuit. Respect for his music continues.

Sonny Murray is native to Brook Village, Inverness County. He also plays the fiddle. He lived in Halifax in the 1950s before settling in Sydney Forks, Cape Breton. Sonny shared the following detail that typically reflects the amazing charisma Buddy had among a generation with post-war opportunities and all that the modern-era music had to offer. Yet Sonny and his close friends in Halifax remained loyal to their musical roots and the music of the Cape Breton fiddler – especially Buddy MacMaster.

Sonny reveals his longstanding regard for Buddy and his music. "I first met Buddy when he came to play for dances at Brook Village ... about 1950 or 1951. I was a teenager at the time. And me being absolutely crazy about the fiddle ... was glued to the stage ... close to the stage while Buddy was playing. What I remember from that time was how nice he was to me ... and I'd be asking about tunes and everything ... I was only a kid but Buddy always took the time to talk to me and tell me the name of the tune. And I never forgot that.

"A few years later I took off to Halifax. I looked up the Cape Breton Club where the fiddlers used to come up for dances. The odd time, of course, Buddy would arrive so I'd be the first one at the hall. Shortly after that I got a job and then I got an old car and a tape recorder ... and the very first live performance that was recorded was at Neilly's in Harbourview (Inverness County) at a dance with Buddy ... and many recordings done over the years with Buddy. He was always very, very generous with his music.

"I even went to his home where his parents treated me like I was very special ... and no matter what was going on there ... haymaking or whatever, it would all seem to stop and everybody came in the house and, of course, they knew we were there for music ... You were treated royally to a meal and then you move into the living room and everything else was forgotten about ... The music started ... I remember Buddy's mother would be reminding him about what to play ... I never forgot those kind of things ... What sticks in my mind ... no matter who came, you were very, very welcome ... and I'm sure they must have had an awful bunch of people bothering them at times but they never showed that way ... Of course, Buddy made tapes there for me, too ...

"In 1959, Margie and I got married and we were very fortunate to have a little house we could rent and where we could have a few parties. [By that time] I was roped into being the entertainer chair at the Cape Breton Club. They wanted dances so the first guy I contacted was Buddy. Up he comes and a great dance, of course. Then the party would start after the dance. And he would play all night for us right through until daybreak.

"So, those were great times for us and this was often, too. And it wasn't just at our house. There was another couple that lived in Halifax in those years – Donald and Isobel Meagher. Donald was from Brook Village. I knew him before I ever left home. And they were crazy about the music. And Buddy would be there sometimes for a party.

"There was another couple from Judique – John and Marcella Beaton. And that was another place to have parties. Buddy never ever refused to go to anyone's house and I'm sure he must have felt like heading to bed after playing all night [at the dance] but he never ever refused anybody to play a tune . . .

"In 1961, the Cape Breton Club wanted to put on a concert in Halifax and they decided they wanted to make a wicked big thing ... Harvey MacDonald from Whycocomagh went and he rented the Halifax Forum ... That scared me half to death because I was on the entertainment committee ... Anyway, him and I came down to Cape Breton and started looking for entertainers ... It seemed it was no trouble at all ... Everyone was rearing to go for the concert ... Of course, our main fiddler was Buddy ... but one of the stars of the show was Cameron Chisholm [a fiddler from Margaree] ... He was just fifteen at the time and I remember he was writing his grade twelve exams and he could just drive right up and they had to get back home ... It was a pretty special thing ... He was a big star of the show along with Buddy, of course ... I can still remember that evening ... is everyone [talent] going to show up? ... The phone rang and it was Buddy ... He was over at his sister Kathleen's already [in Halifax] ... [So] there were no more worries there! There were never any worries about Buddy – he was always there early and no trouble at all ...

"When I finally got some kind of a car that would work half decent, our big goal in life was every Friday evening to get out of Halifax and at least get a couple of sets in Creignish before the dance was over. So, I never left Halifax unless the car was full [with passengers] ... As a matter of fact, one of the girls who travelled with me was Marie Beaton, who is now Buddy's wife ... We're talking in the 1950s before the Trans-Canada Highway ... so it was quite a scurry to get there ... And then the next night – Saturday night – everybody had to be at Neilly's. You just weren't with it unless you all met at Neilly's and it was Buddy again ... and that was a big thing ... I hate to even drive by there now and there's no Neilly's ... that had a great history ... And of course Buddy was the chief all during those years ... John Campbell started there ... but Buddy was the main player that I remember there ... Then when I was on vacation and home, Buddy was playing in Kenloch ... and we'd make a trip down there ... I have a lot of fiddler friends but Buddy is a pretty special one."

While in Mabou, however, Buddy played in the local parish hall often and also got started at the Kenlock hall where he played that dance until the mid-1950s. Buddy explains, "They had great dances there, a lot of good dancers there; it was a real joy to play there. Another place I played a lot at that time was the Labour Temple Hall in Inverness [town]. It was a good big hall with a great dance floor ... They used to come from all over the county for those dances – Judique, Port Hawkesbury, Port Hood, Mabou, Inverness and the Margarees. Everybody would be all dressed up at that time – suits, white shirt and tie; the girls would be all dressed up."

Other locations for dances became available for Buddy as well – Strathlorne, Deepdale, Brook Village, Troy, Scotsville, Long Point and Hawthorne. "A very popular dance scene that began in the early 1950s was at Harbourview. Angus D. MacDonald organized them. His son Neilly took over the dances shortly thereafter. In fact, the hall is often referred to as Neilly's Hall.

"They had a canteen and a little dance hall. I'd say it was around '53. John Campbell played there before I did. John decided to move away to Ontario to seek employment so Angus D. MacDonald approached me to play in John's place ... I was finished playing at the Labour Temple Hall for the Saturday night dances in Inverness."

Paralleling with the early dance scene in Cape Breton were the out-of-town dances. Where Invernessers had migrated in search of work, there was interest in down-home dances. Buddy would be called upon to make frequent trips to key centres to perform. In addition to his Halifax visits, interest in his performances had taken root elsewhere. Opportunities to share his gift of music expanded.

"I'd go to Toronto [organized by Sandy MacIntyre, formerly of Inverness] ... and to Windsor, Ontario," says Buddy. "I used to go up to

Boston to play. Bill Lamey [formerly of River Denys] was in Boston [at] that time and he would get me up ... [at] the Cape Breton Club [and] the Canadian American Club. I played in Sudbury, Ontario, a few times, and then I started to get calls to play in Detroit."

A huge fan of Buddy's music in Detroit is Bobby MacNeil, who has roots in Big Pond, Cape Breton. Bobby lives in Detroit. He was inspired too, by Little Jack MacDonald to learn the violin. Bobby would often frequent Buddy's dances in Detroit. Bobby comments, "Buddy was always a big draw for the dances in the Windsor-Detroit area."

Another staunch Buddy fan is Florence MacMillan, formerly from Inverness County and now living in Windsor, Ontario. She says, "Buddy's dances in Detroit and Windsor are marvelous. Over the years, I looked forward to these dances and seeing so many people from home."

The early Detroit dances were organized by Johnny Archie MacDonald (formerly of Judique), who, as Buddy adds, "played with the Five MacDonald Fiddlers, and he used to get me up to Detroit to play for the Cape Bretoners there."

Music was always part of the MacDonald household in Detroit. Johnny Archie promoted the music in the Detroit area in the 1920s, and he started organizing dances on a small scale with Cape Breton fiddlers living in Detroit. By the 1930s, these dances were often organized as "benefit dances" to provide financial support to Cape Bretoners at home who were struggling and enduring hardship. By the early 1950s, these dances had acquired a note of special social importance and Cape Breton fiddlers were invited often to make the trip to Detroit to perform. The dances were taking place in the off-season, in the fall, winter and spring. The Cape Breton population supporting these dances, including Johnny Archie and family, were always en route to their native homeland in summer. Buddy was very much a part of the dance tradition in Detroit and was always a favourite performer.

Murdoch "Johnny Archie" MacDonald, Johnny Archie's son, was born in Judique but had moved to Detroit as a very young boy with his parents. By that time, Murdoch's father, who was related to Buddy through Buddy's mother, had secured work in Detroit. As a young man, Murdoch returned to Cape Breton. In the spring of 1940 and at the age of seventeen, he was working along the shore near Little Judique with Buddy shovelling gravel onto truck wagons. That began a special friendship that lasts to this day. Murdoch now lives in Washington State on Whidbey Island in Puget Sound.

A particular recollection that Murdoch enjoys sharing is an incident following a dance in Rockport, Maine. Buddy had been invited to perform and asked Murdoch to join him for the road trip. They would be travelling by car. Murdoch says, "On our return, Buddy decided to stop in New Brunswick for Mass. This tall priest was having the Mass. I remember his voice ... so strong and powerful ... At one point, Buddy turned to the person in the pew behind and asked who the priest was ... The name given was a Scottish name. I can't recall it at the moment ... but after Mass, Buddy went to talk to the priest ... What I recall was the manner in which this priest responded to Buddy upon Buddy introducing himself. He was in awe ... I thought the priest was going to go into shock from the surprise at meeting Buddy ... The priest was responding in broken phrases while expressing that he had wished that Buddy had announced in advance that he would be in attendance ... He made a huge fuss over meeting Buddy."

Murdoch's sister, Barbara MacDonald-Magone, however, believes the music was most important. As an accomplished pianist, her special interest in Buddy's music has been life long. She became a close friend and in time accompanied Buddy at the Detroit dances and at many other venues.

Barbara explains, "I was first introduced to him when I was six years old. My father and mother, Dorothy, took a trip to Cape Breton and brought me with them. I guess I went to dances even then, laying contentedly in a bassinette in the back of a parked car right at the door [of the parish hall]. They would check on me in between sets. I'm sure that the music wafted out of the hall and perhaps may have been the very beginning of my love for Cape Breton fiddlers and their music.

"In 1959, we started our annual summer-long trips to Cape Breton from Detroit. We were frequent visitors to John Duncan and Sadie Mac-Master's home, where we always enjoyed wonderful hospitality ... My father continued to collect field recordings and Buddy contributed to his collection every summer. I'm sure Buddy wasn't always in the mood to play when he would arrive home from the Judique railway station, but if he wasn't in the mood, we never knew it. The piano was in the living room, which opened to the dining room. The dining table and buffet were always full of open music books. His sisters, Lorraine and Betty Lou, accompanied him on many of the recordings and when I was older and more accomplished, I was invited to accompany him.

"It was exciting to be in the MacMaster kitchen when Buddy and his sisters were readying themselves for a dance. Buddy would always dress impeccably in a suit and a tie and I remember him always shining his shoes in the kitchen on the edge of the little cot before he left for the dance."

The following story has become legend over the years. Buddy was invited to play in Boston yet again. The arrangements were routine for him: drive from Judique to Halifax in midday with a view to catching a plane for Boston. It was a Friday. All went well in Halifax. Upon his arrival at Logan International Airport, Boston, the usual lineup was waiting – several native Cape Bretoners. Buddy gripped his small carrying case and his fiddle and made his way through the parking lot to a huge car. He took the fiddle with him inside the car.

They had not yet pulled away from the airport when his friends asked immediately that he play a few tunes along the way. And so he did. He arrived at the home where he would spend the evening. He entered the house and again his friends insisted that he play. And so he did. It was now time to head to the dance hall. So, back into the car, where again he kept playing the fiddle until he reached the hall. He played for the entire dance, which went until one o'clock in the morning. Then back into the car to play the fiddle again while making his way to a house session for more music among the Cape Bretoners who have just spent the evening dancing to his music. He played all night and into the wee hours and it was now Saturday morning and time to get back to the airport to make his way to Cape Breton. And so he did – still playing his fiddle. "Buddy, is there no way you can stay another day?" he was asked. "Hell no! I'd love to ... but I have to get home. I'm playing for a dance in Judique tonight," he replied.

Buddy has a wonderful level of energy and stamina for music. Sonny Murray recalls another grueling occasion. "When we moved back to Cape Breton, they had a housewarming for us. It was sort of a surprise ... We were in our first house down the road ... Carl [MacKenzie] was living in Port Hawkesbury and he put the thing together ... Who arrives on the scene, not only Carl, but Estwood Davidson, Winston [Fitzgerald] and Buddy. It was just before that time that Buddy had a misfortune and hurt his arm ... I forget the details but he had a cast on for awhile and this was the first night that he was able to play. So, he came to the house ... and of course, the humble Buddy ... 'Well I don't know if I can play ... can't do very much, you know.' But, by gosh [he laughs] the arm got a great workout, I'll tell you, that night.

"Buddy had come down with Joe 'Tac' MacDougall ... and when he went home there was some mixup with the jacket. He took Carl's jacket [by mistake] ... and [Carl's] car keys were in it ... Next day when he got up to go to church he realized he had Carl's car keys ... and [thinks Carl] is stranded [at Sonny's] ... but really Carl was not stranded but thank goodness that Buddy thought that ... because we sat down to lunch ... rap on the door and there's himself again ... Well, that was the greatest afternoon ... that sticks out in my mind ... Carl and I were talking about that not too long ago ... After dinner was had, the two of them sat down in the living room and they played right into the evening sometime. It was just fantastic. I have a lot of very fond memories of good times with Buddy. He is a good friend."

The dance settings at which Buddy is comfortable and appears to enjoy the most are the dances that take place very near his home in Judique. Buddy is a legend to many dancers throughout Cape Breton but certain locations do stand out as being near and dear to his heart. Another appealing spot on the horizon was the new Glendale Hall beginning in 1965. Buddy comments, "I can't remember the year the hall was built ... but they had different players. Then [the parish priest] Father John Angus Rankin approached me to play there on a regular basis, so I agreed. They were great dances too."

But the one dance hall in Cape Breton that caught the attention of all of Buddy's dance music enthusiasts was at Glencoe Mills – for over thirty years. It seemed to have special magic. Despite the wonderful journey Buddy had with his dance music by this time, he still had no huge expectation or demands on the people who organized dances in the tiny rural communities. He would gladly accept the invitation to perform on a regular basis and made do with whatever resources or lack of resources he faced in the halls throughout Inverness County. Staging was not always up to speed. The sound systems were inadequate and the poor condition of the pianos was evident in many places. This was the case in Glencoe Mills when the dances were first being planned.

Glencoe Mills is a small community in Inverness County. It is encircled to the north by Hillsboro, to the southwest by Mabou River, to the west by Port Hood, to the south by River Denys and to the east by Whycocomagh. In an earlier generation, the area provided its inhabitants with fertile land for farming and sufficient lumber for three sawmills at one time. John L. MacDougall wrote in 1922, "In the pioneer days, [Glencoe] must have looked forbidding and wild. But the scene has changed. Not many rural communities can surpass it today in its cultivation and prosperity. All honour to the stout hearts and strong hands who have wrought the happy change."

Time, however, would challenge Glencoe Mills, as it has other small communities. It began to suffer from out-migration by the next generation. Young people left the diehards to preserve some of the community that once was. Many jest that on Sundays there are more parishioners in the graveyard than inside the church for Mass. Nevertheless, like other small communities, the residents would persevere throughout the 1970s and 1980s, and Buddy MacMaster would be a contributing factor. For more than thirty years, during the summer months, Buddy was the regular fiddler at the hall in Glencoe on Thursday evenings. His ability to draw a capacity crowd enabled the sponsor – the church – to generate a cash flow that otherwise may not have been so easily available.

Emily Addison writes, "The dances are important to the operation of the church in Glencoe. The dances and a few other fundraisers complement the income that is donated by the small number of families in the parish. In 1999, the square dances in Glencoe raised $10,167. ... [T]he money raised goes towards the upkeep of the church, the hall and the grounds."

Buddy recalls, "They converted the Glencoe School into a recreation building ... They asked me to play there. I agreed and it went very well ... The people of the community really supported it. Everyone would go to the dance, so they had a great time and with a crowd like that the people from the surrounding areas would go as well."

Joey Beaton is a celebrated pianist from Mabou. He is the son of pianist Elizabeth Beaton and Cape Breton fiddler/composer the late Donald Angus Beaton. Joey would often accompany Buddy at these dances. Joey collects and researches information about the music tradition. He taped an interview with Buddy about the Glencoe Dances for the Inverness County Archives in 1993. During the course of the interview, Joey invited Buddy to spend a few moments reflecting on the more humorous aspects of the early Glencoe dances.

Buddy: I can recall quite vividly ... they didn't have a piano. They borrowed an organ from Mary Fountain, one of these old-fashioned pump organs.

Joey: I know. I was exhausted by the end of the dance.

Buddy: We were kind of laughing ... getting a kick out of the whole thing anyway. There was a large crowd.

Joey: Packed hall.

Buddy: I think that we were so pleased that everyone was having such a good time.

Joey: Then they tried to improve the situation, Buddy. What did they do after that?

Buddy: They built a little place for us. A little cubbyhole and that was small but still it separated us from the dancers. We were elevated a little higher from the floor.

Joey: There was only room for you, Joe "Tac" MacDougall and myself. We used to have a lot of fun on that stage ... good memories, Buddy. Hughie "Donald Hughie" used to come up and make some announcements ... We used to get just a charge out of those announce-

Joey Beaton, Buddy MacMaster and the legendary Glencoe Mills Hall.

Joey Beaton and Buddy on stage at the Glencoe Mills Hall in the early 1990s.

The Buddy MacMaster smile.

ments. ... They went to Sydney and bought an upright piano. That was quite an improvement.

The regular Thursday night dance with Buddy attracted people from far and near. Margaret Dunn, formerly of Glendale, Cape Breton, and now of Antigonish, has a wonderful reputation as one of Cape Breton's outstanding step dancers. Margaret, like so many of her contemporaries, made many visits to the Glencoe Hall over the years. She shared a wonderful story about the level of enthusiasm she personally witnessed concerning Buddy and Glencoe.

A young woman with European roots was living in the States. She had received information about the Cape Breton square dance scene from some source and had heard in particular about the Glencoe Mills dance. She hitchhiked to Canada and made her way to Halifax. From there, she made contact with Margaret. She asked for directions to Glencoe – still hitching. At some point, she realized she would arrive in Judique first. So she decided to locate Buddy's home. Her doggedness paid off and she knocked on Buddy's door. He already had several people in his kitchen who were waiting for a drive to Glencoe. Buddy opened the door and was greeted by this strange woman. He offered her a cup of tea and agreed to give her a ride to the dance. They all made their way to Glencoe Mills.

How does one get to Glencoe? Natalie MacMaster, a celebrated fiddler and Buddy's niece, has been asked this question on many occasions in her travels. She gives directions in the liner notes of her CD *Natalie MacMaster Live*, released in 2002: "You'll go over the causeway around the rotary, take a sharp left down Route 19 and keep driving. You'll eventually come to a sign that says Glencoe Mills. Take a right and keep driving until the pavement ends. You'll come to a fork in the road, take a right and go over the one lane bridge. Keep driving (it'll be dark now). You'll pass a house ... keep driving. You'll eventually see a light and a little hall and you'll hear the music. Now you've reached the square dance in Glencoe."

There are many roads to Glencoe Mills. Fred White describes how he got to Glencoe: "I was travelling with a friend, a huge Buddy fan. This was my first visit to Glencoe Mills, and it was a daunting experience. We turned off at the 125 at Vi's Restaurant in Whycocomagh and drove to the dirt road that intersects the pavement on the left. We turned left and headed west. I think it was west; it may have been south. I really didn't know.

"At first I recalled seeing the odd house here and there on either side. As we drove further, large piles of pulpwood appeared, stacked on either side of the road; there were a series of smaller roads on the sides, too. I presumed that these were to access pulpwood and, at one time, for connecting the many small rural communities, typical of many areas of rural Cape Breton. As we drove on, the houses were less frequent. There was not another sign of human activity. It was now starting to get a bit dark and still no sign of a dance hall. I don't recall seeing other cars on the road either.

"Although I did not express my thoughts to my friend, at this time, a bit of doubt was creeping into my mind. I started to wonder whether he really knew where he was going. I tried to guess how long we had been driving since we left the paved road to estimate how far we had come. It had been some time since we had seen the last house, and I had some doubt that a hall with any type of dance and crowd would exist in this setting.

"Just as I was about to suggest maybe we were on the wrong road, a small opening appears in the woods. By this time it is mostly dark and a single light bulb on a pole illuminates the outline of a structure that stands in the opening. My friend eagerly announces, 'Here we are!'"

The countywide dance scene was operating on meagre resources. There were limited dollars for facilities and advertisement and the performance fees were certainly not lucrative for the fiddlers, including Buddy, but as was the case with many of the fiddlers, the money was secondary to him. He was very aware that in some playing engagements the money promised might not be available. This could be for any number of reasons – small crowds due to competition from other events or poor weather conditions. It may have been that Buddy would want to make a contribution to the fundraising dances and, therefore, he would often leave his fee at the door. His expression of generosity when the sponsor was faced with these types of conditions was commonly understood and has been felt across the county and beyond. But some always feel that he was making a huge sum of money between working with CN and the slew of dances and concerts.

One particular story has Buddy being pestered on matters of money by a local gentleman during his early dance routine. John Donald Cameron tells the story nicely.

"In the late 1940s and the early 1950s, [Buddy] was playing at a lot of dances. There was this particular gentleman who used to come into the station [in Mabou] often and talk. 'You must be making an awful lot of money. You're working in here, you're working in the railroad and you're playing for dances and everything.' He kept on doing this. Anyway, Buddy was getting kind of tired of this kind of talk, because he did not get paid for every dance he played at ... So one day he decided to play a trick on this fellow. [The fellow made his usual visit to the station and asked,] 'Well, where were you playing last night?' Buddy told him ... 'Well, boy, you're making money. Aren't you?' Buddy's reply was, 'As a matter of fact, I am ... Here's my billfold' ... So, he took out his billfold ... he had put a fifty dollar bill on each side of a roll of Robin Hood stuff [coupons] ... and an elastic around [it] ... 'That's what I have been making ... I've been saving for Christmas.' Well, [the man's] eyes were kind of googley and that was the end of that ... There was no more said about that, you know."

Addressing the inadequate sound systems in the local halls in particular would rest with the fiddlers eventually. Buddy has his own recollections of efforts to acquire a sound system so the dancing was more enjoyable. "To carry the music [without amplification] you had to have two fiddlers [for increased volume]. That's how it was done. The first fiddlers around here to have an amplifier were the Lewis [MacDonald] Boys. Winston [Fitzgerald] was going strong then and he had a system. When I came to Mabou [1949], I decided to get one, too. There was a fellow in Inverness ... Vern MacLeod ... he had a ham radio in his house ... and he could get all that stuff on a good deal. I got a system from him ... It was pretty sophisticated for its time ... I did not have the money myself ... I went to the Royal Bank to borrow some money to buy the system ... They were awfully strict there ... I could not get the money for that purpose ... so, that did not stop me ... I don't remember what

I did ... but I got a system. Up until then I was borrowing a system. It was required for the Labour Temple Hall in Inverness ... That was a big hall."

Buddy speaks with pride about the old "horn" sound system. He had purchased it sometime in the 1960s. It was a distinguishing feature at the time. It was compact to carry around and to set up. He would perch it on top of the piano wherever he was playing. The sound would carry over the heads of the dance crowd whether the hall was big or small. The system is still in his basement at his home.

"A young fellow from Ontario was attending one of the dances ... maybe it was Glendale ... I can't recall ... He took notice of the old horn sitting on the top of the piano. He said to me that the system looked like an old antique. I said it may well be an antique ... but it has good sound." [Buddy laughs.]

Buddy recalls a rather abrupt visit by a dear friend to the hall to see his new system. "I was playing some jigs for a set. There was a large crowd. I could see him coming. He waved as he made his way toward the stage. He kept bumping the dancers. But he was excited about my system and he wanted to see it. He was having a few, you know. But I knew he would be no bother. But as he made his way on the stage he slipped and fell backwards. As he did, his left heel went into the air just before he began tumbling down the steps. He kicked the old horn accidentally, of course, and it rattled a bit. It didn't fall but he left a huge dent on the horn. ... Oh, I just kept playing. I was in the middle of a set, you know. And a bunch a people helped him. He was okay. But the dent is still on the horn." [He laughs.]

Buddy upgraded from his reliable horn to a more modern system that has both disadvantages and advantages. "I think it was $1,200. I've had it a number of years now. The speakers are heavy. Of course, all those speakers are heavy. The weather does not affect them ... and there are no dents so far!"

Joey Beaton concludes his interview about the recollections of the Glencoe dances with the following tribute to his good friend Buddy. "From 1965-66 through to 1993, the Glencoe dances have just made a tremendous name for themselves. Your outstanding fiddling has certainly brought people from all over Canada, the United States, the Scottish homeland

and I hope that the Glencoe dances will live on for many, many years more."

Although Buddy has not played in Glencoe on a regular basis now for several years, the fond memories of his performances there will live on for years to come.

Buddy MacMaster's contribution between 1950 and 1975 to the music tradition was particularly significant. In an earlier era, Decca and Celtic released 78s in the 1920s and 1930s by several Cape Breton musicians. And the private radio productions by CJCB in Syndey and CJFX in Antigonish were especially important in keeping the music alive. With the exception of the field recordings of Buddy by CJFX Radio, records and radio were less significant in how the public came to appreciate Buddy's music. Furthermore, Buddy made the choice to focus on the live dance tradition. He especially helped to keep the music and the dance active at home and away. He offered a venue that was much more participatory for the people – to dance. The recordings and the radio outlets were more passive. For the fiddler, of course, radio and records were very important to developing the music and passing along new tunes. Buddy's part in the tradition provided a real opportunity for people to fully socialize and to enjoy the music. Nevertheless, Buddy was fighting the odds.

The dance culture experienced a drastic change in the mid-1960s. This prevailed until the mid-1970s. The presence of the fiddler at the local hall was less prevalent. Jimmy MacInnis offers the following comments concerning the era when dances were beginning to have less appeal in the Inverness County community.

"I remember going to Judique and the fiddler was not the main thing in our era [the early 1960s] ... There were the Beatles, the Stones, and then the pig-n-whistles took over ... See, my older brothers did not see the liquor at the dances [inside the dance halls] ... I could go with my brothers when I was fifteen to a dance ... Then with the pig-n-whistles [cash bar becomes popular] ... there was a generation who never got to go with older brothers, mothers, fathers, whatever ... so they never got to experience that. They would attend the teen dances instead ... That was a bad era when the young and the old were not going together ... The dances dropped eventually. That's when the fiddle began to die except for Glencoe ... Through all that time, Buddy was a [living] legend."

Margie MacInnis comments, "When we were in grade eleven and twelve, most people were going to rock and roll dances ... but we liked to go to the fiddle dances, at Glencoe especially. So we wouldn't have a drive, so we'd call Buddy ... He'd say, 'Oh, come up with me.' We'd walk up to his place and leave [with Buddy] at 8:30 for Glencoe ... I lived about a half mile from Buddy. [Jimmy interjects, suggesting that the real interest on the part of Margie and her friends in Glencoe was that the Mabou guys might be there.] ... Very few of our era that age were going to the square dances ... Like when I would go back to school on Monday and tell them that I went to the square dance ... they weren't as impressed as if you'd tell them that you went to one of the rock concerts."

The summer scene did keep the square dancing active in some places, but it is fair to say that the square dance scene in greater Cape Breton has not fully recovered from its demise in that earlier era.

Jimmy and Margie MacInnis now live in West Mabou. In 1988, to bridge the ever-widening generation gap, they began the family square dance program in the West Mabou Hall. The dances are still popular to this day. The West Mabou program is a weekly year-round venue. The dances are a way to raise money for local sport teams.

However, Jimmy and Margie made a few adjustments to the dance tradition. They decided that it is best to invite different fiddlers to perform at the dances – in other words, to not restrict the dance to the same fiddler on a weekly basis. There are several reasons for this approach. One is economics. Some fiddlers simply cost more to hire than others. This would allow many of the fiddlers who were younger and looking for playing experience to perform at dances at the West Mabou Hall – Kimberley Fraser, Neil Beaton and Jackie Dunn, to name a few. There were fewer restrictions on the dance style itself, as the prompter or caller was not to be a feature at West Mabou. The dancers had a free-for-all and the number of couples in a set was limitless, but still fun. The idea that the dance was open to all ages was important as well. This would address the need for the younger generation to join with the older generation if the dance tradition was to survive. The MacInnises opted not to offer a cash bar.

Lorrie MacKinnon is from Oakville, Ontario. Her grandmother was born at Long Point, grew up in Port Hood and was a descendent of the Creignish MacMasters – Ian (Ruadh) MacMaster who settled in Creignish and who, upon his arrival from Scotland in 1801, had built the stone house that still stands today. His first cousin was Donald MacMaster, the weaver, from whom Buddy's people are descended. Lorrie's grandfather was from Maryvale, Antigonish County. The late Gus MacKinnon, well-known announcer and promoter of Cape Breton fiddling at CJFX, is a relation.

Lorrie attended dances in Mississauga and Toronto, Ontario, in the early 1990s. Alexander MacDonnell and Carl Beaton had organized a schedule of about two dances a month. Both men are very well entrenched in the Cape Breton music tradition as they are formerly from Mabou. Alexander is a celebrated stepdancer, and Carl has strong musical ties with Mabou.

Lorrie first heard Buddy perform in 1991 at the Union Hall dance in Mississauga. Her comments indicate the expatriate Cape Bretoners in Toronto and area were continuing the tradition that had begun many years earlier in places like Halifax, Boston and Detroit. But they too were experiencing some change from the earlier dance format. Once again, though, Buddy would persevere.

Lorrie reflects, "They would bring fiddlers up ... At that time there were many young fiddlers they were starting to showcase ... People would come from all over the place ... mostly expatriate Cape Bretoners ... There were people who were loyal and they would come out no matter what. Then there were people that would only come if certain fiddlers were there ... So on the one hand that was great because they knew if they brought up ... Natalie MacMaster or Buddy MacMaster in particular ... they would get a really good turn out . . .

"The dances ... would also have a DJ ... so they would play one set and then the DJ would play for twenty minutes ... rock and roll, country ... like being at a wedding ... Also, the third turn [figure] they would cut it short ... So the third turn was not nearly as fun as when it was done right through ...

"You could always count on a crowd when Buddy came up ... They come from Windsor, Detroit ... a group would come down from Sudbury and people were excited ... People [from the Ottawa Valley] who were learning to play fiddle would always come out for Buddy . . .

"In between the turns [figures], everybody would be clambering the stage to talk to Buddy. He was always so gracious and he knew everybody. If you met him once, he would remember who you were and he was so glad to see them ... and it must have been so exhausting because he would be put to work as well. He was expected to play at a party afterward till all hours and so he played practically all night and then have breakfast and go to Mass and then go home [to Cape Breton] ... and so in some way it was a very exhausting trip for him but he always came when he was asked, if he could ... There was always an excitement about his being there."

Buddy found himself in the midst of change within the dance tradition on earlier occasions. His visits to Boston, following an absence because of his busy playing schedule elsewhere, were similar to the situation in Mississauga and Toronto in the early 1990s described by Lorrie MacKinnon. In 1989, Buddy was coerced to renew appearances by a good friend to the music and the dance tradition in the greater Boston area, Gabe Arsenault.

Before moving to Boston, Gabe had acquired a respect and love for the music from his youthful days growing up in Belle Cote, Inverness County, where he lived as a young boy, often rushing home from school to listen to the music on radio or television.

Gabe had organized dances at the Canadian-American and the French clubs. He was an old hat at the game. "My first dance was with Theresa MacLellan in 1972 or 1973. I started the dances because I loved the music. Then I got Jerry Holland ... then I got Donnie LeBlanc ... then I got Howie MacDonald. But by 1989, I was pretty steady with Buddy, almost every year. To please the people, we would play the Boston set and then follow that with the Mabou set." Interestingly, the format described by Lorrie MacKinnon may help explain, according to Gabe, why the Boston dance scene still is able to keep the sets to a minimum number of couples. It would appear that it is difficult to enter the Boston set easily, and he explains that this reluctance carries into the Mabou sets that are danced, keeping the Mabou sets to four couples.

When asked how important it was to have Buddy perform at these dances, Gabe explains, "Well, Buddy always drew a crowd; everyone loves him. They love his music and his personality. The older people would come out for Buddy when they would not come for anyone else. Older people would always talk to him. He is keeping it steady [the dance tradition]. [And] he is a fair man. I'd always try to give him an extra bit, but he would not take it. I'd find it on the bureau after he'd leave my place for home."

Gabe observes that the dance scene today is attracting a greater number of Americans to the halls in Boston. The 1990s saw enthusiasts from as far away as Texas and as nearby as Maine travel to the dances. Buddy and select young fiddlers, especially Ashley MacIsaac, were in the midst of this. Gabe adds, "Buddy drew the crowd from all over." He laments that the younger generation in the Boston area with Cape Breton roots do not seem to have the same level of interest as in the past and without the American interest, the dances would not be viable financially. Gabe further observes that the Cape Bretoners are now less inclined to make their way from home (Cape Breton) to attend Boston dances, recalling this was a strong feature of the Boston dances in the past. "The dance scene is not a money-making enterprise. The only reason I do it is for the love of the music and to keep it. To see people dancing makes me happy. You have no idea of the number of people I met because of Scotch music."

Buddy's remarkable dance circuit throughout Cape Breton and in major centres in other parts of Canada and the U.S. has contributed to the longevity of the music tradition as well as the dance. He had been called upon to perform from a very young age through to his more senior years. He always accepted an invitation to perform at a dance, whether it was in the local Judique hall or a major venue in California. Through his network, countless people have been affected by his music. He has inspired young and old to carry on the music tradition. His legacy to the Cape Breton dance tradition will remain for many years to come.

Home and Community

In 1968, Buddy MacMaster had decided he would marry, and so he did. Buddy had known his bride-to-be, Marie Beaton, for several years; she would frequent the dances at which he played. At the time and to this day, Marie, the daughter of Hugh and Anne Beaton, always claims that she hailed from the capital of Judique, and that is "Little Judique." On November 9, 1968, Buddy and Marie were married at St. Peter's Church in Port Hood. They subsequently had two children, Mary Elizabeth, born in 1972 (she currently resides in Mabou with her husband John and their four children), and Allan Gerard, born in 1974 (he currently resides in Halifax). Marie explains that she understood that music would always be part of the family. She understood as well that Buddy had an extremely busy schedule with community commitments, council meetings, family and music. In fact, by the mid-1960s, Buddy MacMaster's reputation as a popular musician and highly respected citizen of the greater community of Judique gave some the idea he might serve the community in other ways.

Over the years, Buddy was appointed to several provincial boards and was elected to public office. He served on the board of directors for Sysco, the Sydney Steel Corporation, with an appointment on June 26, 1984, which was renewed for a second term in November 1988. In 1985, he was named to the Canso Regional Vocational School Board and reappointed in 1988.

He felt prepared for these appointments. By 1968, Buddy was an elected councillor for the Municipality of the County of Inverness. This was at a time when the tides for new development were beginning to take hold. But he had no illusions that things were going to move quickly simply because he was now on council. For example, during his tenure he participated in discussions concerning a proposed causeway link between Port Hood Island and Port Hood. Those discussions had been underway since 1904 – even prior to the talks leading up to development of the Canso Causeway, which opened in 1955. There is no indication even in 2007 that a causeway will ever be built. Boat tours from Little Judique Harbour still take visitors to Port Hood Island and offer an opportunity to see whales and bald eagles.

Nevertheless, as Council minutes of 1968-75 show, these were times of challenge for all residents and especially for those who had been elected to represent the interests of the diverse community of Inverness County consisting primarily of Scots, Acadians and First Nations. Although the latter were not represented on council, many of the decisions taken by council would have had an impact on the First Nations people, as a regional development plan had been widely discussed and then adopted by council in March 1969. Furthermore, the former town of Inverness itself had only been designated a district in 1969 and was now aligned with the political structure of the wider county. The Inverness Development Association was now organized with a view to "making new progress." Subsequently, the Industrial Promotion Committee was established for the purpose of "promotion of industry and other resources of the council."

There were many issues that faced Inverness County, such as the need to install a new dial telephone system, a "comprehensive" high school for Central Inverness, additional school amalgamation and construction, and expanded highway construction in the interest of tourism, thus maintaining the county as a gateway to the Cabot Trail. One county councillor emphasized, "It is essential that the county keep pace with improvements; otherwise, there is a danger of the County of Inverness being bypassed when the Louisbourg Restoration project is completed."

There were lively discussions to locate a provincial park for the Mabou-Inverness highway. More specific to Buddy's district, he did advocate the idea that the Judique-Habourview Shore Road be properly paved. He made a case in the interest of the local school buses, the traffic around the fishing ports and the arrival of new homes in the area.

Of the sometimes heated discussions, Buddy remarks, "There were moments at council when I thought I was back at the old dance halls and watching the build-up to those fisticuffs. But in the end, we always managed to settle things in the proper way."

During his tenure, he was appointed to several committees of council. By February 1970, he was on the License and Ferries Committee and the Public Accounts Committee. In May 1970, he was on the Regional Planning Committee. Shortly thereafter, he was named to the executive of the Civil Defense and Welfare Committees. In 1971, Buddy was appointed to the then Municipal School Board and the issue of amalgamation was on the top of the list for discussion. In the same year, he was on the Recreation Committee. He had expressed his support for vital issues to the community at large, including the idea of a park in the Cape Mabou-Sight Point area. He endorsed the Beaches Protection Act of Nova Scotia. That act is under considerable review today by area residents located near beaches.

In the early 1970s, an important issue for County Council was to encourage efforts to revitalize the Gaelic language, island-wide. Inverness County was now on the verge of awakening to the tremendous possibilities for Gaelic retention – through education, heritage awareness and a wide range of cultural initiatives that would form the basis of the exciting activities now in place along Route 19. One motion at council read, "Council [should] endorse efforts to have a Cape Breton bilingual and bicultural nature emphasis by erecting bilingual Gaelic-English road signs on the Cape Breton highway, at the Canso Causeway and in private and municipal jurisdictions to the extent that is practical and economically feasible." Buddy was in the thick of those discussions.

Thankfully, perserverance prevails. The December 8, 2006, edition of the *Cape Breton Post* had an article entitled, "Inverness County hoping to feature road signs in both Gaelic and English." The article states, "Municipal council has passed a resolution calling for the installation of road signs featuring the Gaelic language to greet people as they enter and leave the communities of Mabou and Inverness." Buddy is probably whispering, "*Tha mi toilichte a nis. Suas leis a Gaidhlig.*" (I am happy now. Up with the Gaelic language.)

The entertainment business and tourism generally would now play a significant role at council. By 1973, for example, council was actively supporting the preparation for the first ever Festival of Cape Breton Scottish Fiddlers. So a new era for music had emerged and, where possible, it was to be appreciated not only as a local heritage but also as a way to support local business.

Buddy engaged in some old-time politics between tunes and council meetings. His participation at council was at a time when the standard political party lines were clear within all the county districts. In fact, provincial party politics in Nova Scotia at that time was organized on the basis of county districts, and nominating committees within the districts, tied to the provincial network, selected the candidates to run for council elections. It was accepted that certain longstanding traditions and practices be maintained. Therefore, political patronage, for example, was expected to remain an integral feature of the provincial-county network in each district. It was no different in Inverness County.

Judique (District Two), like other districts in the County of Inverness, had its own executives and chairpersons who were involved in the affairs of the old guard parties – Liberals and Conservatives in particular. Yet, despite the potential for entrenchment by the people along the same party lines, it was understood that the municipal council was one level in politics where the electorate were marginally prepared to move from one political stripe to another. The candidates, however, and subsequently the elected representatives of council were perceived to unofficially be Strong Tories or Big Liberals. One significant impact this tradition had on County Council directly was that the majority vote on council (Liberal or Conservative) would carry the vote to appoint the County Warden.

By 1967, it was understood that Buddy was a Liberal – but the con-

Buddy and Marie MacMaster's wedding, November 9, 1968, at St. Peter's Church in Port Hood.

The MacMaster family: Buddy, Mary Elizabeth, Marie and Allan.

Dr. Buddy MacMaster proudly displays his "X" ring (1995) from St. Francis Xavier University.

Buddy with his sister Jeannie as they reminisce family stories.

Buddy's parents, John Duncan and Sarah MacMaster celebrate their fiftieth wedding anniversary in 1970 with Father Hugh D. MacDonald.

sensus appears that he was neither a Big Liberal nor a Strong Liberal. It is fair to say that his affiliation with the Liberal Party, however, would have helped him get elected to council in the first place. Over the years, as he served on council, his dedication to the cause of community was not an issue and this is well documented. His increasing demand, however, as a musician during his tenure as a councillor was on the increase and so this was a concern for some. Would he be able to manage the two – council and music – in addition to his full-time work as an employee with CN?

What was apparent to some was that the Liberal Party expected Buddy to possibly move into provincial politics eventually. He was, after all, an immensely popular individual in his community and beyond. But some political forces within the party felt that the dilemma concerning his music had to be resolved. Thus, for some, Buddy's performance schedule as a musician would certainly be a factor in determining the level of support he would garnish from the Liberal Party within the district. In the end, despite his good efforts on council, the Liberal network was determined that it could not have the distraction of an active world-class musician as a part-time politician.

Danny Graham from Judique acquired a passion for politics at an early age. As a young eighteen-year-old, he attended a rally for the future Prime Minister of Canada – Pierre Elliot Trudeau – in the town of Port Hawkesbury in 1968. Trudeau-mania was just beginning to take hold. In later years, Danny became a successful candidate himself in provincial politics, having run for the Liberals in Inverness South in 1988. He left the House of Assembly in 1993 and has known Buddy all his life.

One particular year offered a most memorable county election. Danny's father, Alex, had been released from hospital and, still recovering from surgery on election day, was not able to vote. According to Danny, his father was okay with that. Danny explains this had everything to do with backroom politics in the district and Buddy's performing duties as a fiddler. The politics of the day had been clearly shaped by the Liberal Party long before election day.

Danny remembers, "Buddy was a very busy man at the time with his music. His music took him away from the area a lot. There were some who felt that he was not as accessible as they would have liked. And he was ahead of his time too, as he was not a big believer in the patronage system.

"As a result, at one nominating committee meeting, the Liberals decided to go with another candidate for council. As it happened, the individual that was nominated was not able to run because of a technicality. So they asked Jerome Gillis [a friend and neighbour of Danny's father] who had been a councillor on a previous occasion to run. The strategy clearly was to displace Buddy on Council. The Warden [Walter Moore] at the time was extremely upset that Buddy was defeated [in committee]. He spoke out very strongly about what had happened. Buddy ran as an Independent. My father was in a very tight spot. Jerome Gillis was his first door neighbour and Buddy was his very good friend.

"Buddy didn't win that election, not because people had anything against him personally, but rather it was the old Liberal-Tory issue. The Liberals [in the district of Judique] were voting for the perceived Liberal candidate [Jerome Gillis]. Buddy did very well, however. The election was very close. But Buddy did feel that the Liberal Party mistreated him. I can relate to that myself. [Danny laughs.] It took a little while but Buddy then decided to join the Tory Party. That's the way it took place in my memory."

Meddling is something that Buddy experiences in the music scene as well. He is reluctant to discuss meddling in any context; in fact, he seldom will. He did share the following, but his story requires some background.

From time to time, local musicians, like politicians, feel they have claim to certain territory. Some feel that select areas belong to them. They should have first dibs on playing the dance or concert – whatever the case may be. This has caused some peculiar behaviour among some musicians and even diehard fans. In music as it was in politics, Buddy has been the victim of rather interesting efforts by some.

"Well, I was asked to play at this dance one time in a certain community. It is located a fair distance from Judique ... about a two-hour drive, I guess. Anyway, someone thought that I was interfering ... or something.

I don't really know. But anyway, someone called my home the day of the dance and said the dance was cancelled. I never thought anymore of it. The weather was really bad so I could see cancelling. Later, I was sitting at the table and having my supper ... I got a call from the gentleman who had actually booked me for the dance letting me know that I was welcome to stay overnight. . . as the weather was not so good. I explained about the call I had gotten earlier. He was very surprised and said that the dance was definitely on. Anyway, I finished my supper and grabbed my fiddle and headed for the dance. It was a great dance. I guess that was one time when the bad weather helped a dance."

Situations like the above story and politics in general do not change Buddy's personality. He is consistent with his disposition towards people. In 1966, on their way to Judique, Buddy and John Allan Cameron made an unplanned visit to a home in Big Pond, where Buddy had been before for music sessions. The place was filled with kids but there was a definite interest in the household in the music.

Christie MacInnis vividly recalls the visit: "It was just beginning to get dark. I could see a car coming along the driveway. I was just not prepared for them. One of the kids had the flu. I remember that. There was only the stuff in that we would eat. I know I didn't have a single sweet to give with the tea and there was no store for a couple of miles. It was closed by that time anyway.

"But they came in and made themselves at home and without hesitation started playing music. The music was terrific. I remember that, too. At some point Buddy could hear me continually apologizing for not having something good for tea. 'The tea is good enough,' they kept saying. Later, Buddy called me aside. 'Now don't you be worrying. I am just like you people. I may have made a name for myself with the fiddle but that's it. So never you mind and just enjoy and don't be worrying about anything.' He made me feel so comfortable."

Now back to the Liberal politics of 1975. Not all Liberals were going to be so quick to let Buddy MacMaster lose. Some were prepared to keep him in their sights and not let him get too far away – fiddle or no fiddle. Among the more shrewd politicians of the day from Inverness County was the always formidable Allan J. MacEachen, former Deputy Prime Minister of Canada. While serving as Secretary of State for External Affairs in the Trudeau cabinet in 1975, he was asked by officials in the High Commission in Britain to assemble a worthy cast of Nova Scotia musicians to present a ceilidh at Edinburgh Castle, Scotland. It would be the first ever official ceilidh to take place inside the castle. He made arrangements for some of the best from Nova Scotia to make the journey to the Old Country. Among the musicians MacEachen invited was Buddy MacMaster.

Thus, new doors opened for Buddy, not on council, which he left in 1974, but rather on stage. This was not something that he had pursued. Rather, a new audience was now to discover the wonderful musical skill of this musician who had played his music to that point primarily in Cape Breton and areas that had a direct link with Cape Breton. That would change. Buddy would take to the stage in a manner that would be different and even more demanding of his time and talent.

Despite efforts to keep Buddy Liberal, he developed a closer link with the Conservative Party of Nova Scotia, however. In 1999, Allan MacMaster, Buddy's son, was appointed executive assistant to Rodney MacDonald, who was then Minister of Tourism, Culture and Heritage for the Province of Nova Scotia. In 2006, Rodney MacDonald became Leader of the Progressive Conservative Party and the twenty-sixth Premier of the Province of Nova Scotia.

Musical Influences

Buddy MacMaster's powerful music performances evolved from a deep link with the music tradition that was so much a part of his youth. He has an immensely rich background in the culture.

Buddy's sisters are excellent exponents of the music tradition. They enjoy music through piano, song and dance. His daughter Mary Elizabeth is an accomplished pianist and his niece Natalie MacMaster is an international star performer.

Buddy's brother Alex (Natalie's father) is no less a character than Buddy. He is very talented and witty. If it's possible, he is more modest than Buddy. This delightful little story has followed him in his lifetime: whenever asked if he plays the fiddle, Alex's reply is, "Of course." When asked if he'll play a tune, Alex's reply is always, "I don't think so – not today." And when asked why, his reply is always the same: "I don't want to spoil my reputation."

Doug MacPhee is a close friend of Buddy's and an accomplished pianist. He is also an authority on the Cape Breton music tradition. Buddy and Doug travelled together and performed at different venues and many house sessions over the years. Doug says, "His sisters are all great players and they know Buddy so well from having played at home with him for years. Kathleen was likely the sister who played first with Buddy at the early house sessions, as she is the oldest in the family and played at the old time picnics in the county. The sisters know exactly what he likes from a piano player. They were very good when they teamed up with Buddy.

"When I first began to hear Buddy in person in the late '40s and early '50s, it was Genevieve who was performing with him. They were a great team. I know in later years Lorraine played on a regular basis at the dances. In fact, one of my special recollections of an outstanding music session with Buddy was in the early '70s at Lorraine's home in Port Hawkesbury. Buddy was just amazing there, as was Lorraine. Of course, Betty [Lou] was often with him in later years too, especially at the Glendale and Glencoe dances. She knew his music like a book. She was as steady as a rock and that is important to Buddy."

Buddy comments on what he appreciates in piano accompaniment. "We have so many great piano players in Cape Breton. I enjoy all the piano players, of course. They do not often get the full recognition that they deserve. And they all have their own unique style, too ... but I enjoy a piano player who has life in their music. That helps me to try and be lively. I like them to have some lift ... that they should have good timing and not rush especially when playing for dancers ... square dancers and stepdancers. That's important ... but I like when they don't force the music either. So there is a balance at play and that makes for good accompaniment ... Fiddlers usually take the lead. That's what I enjoy in piano players anyway. But I believe different fiddlers look for different things. And that's good, too."

Doug MacPhee shares the following view: "John Morris Rankin was wonderful with Buddy. He had a great lift in his music. Joey Beaton is very, very good with him, too. His own daughter Mary Elizabeth played in recent years. She is very good. In a recording Buddy did a few years ago, he performed with at least a dozen different piano players. He featured a different player on each cut. It was a wonderful tribute to the piano players to be with him on the recording. I felt honoured to have been invited. Buddy always presented a challenge for whoever was accompanying him. It is and was always a tall order. You had to be on your toes. He is so alert himself and so aware. He gives full attention and looks for that among piano players, too."

The encouragement provided by all piano players, including his siblings, has been important to Buddy. They have contributed to his stamina and commitment to the tradition and this has enabled Buddy to develop a high level of confidence, poise, consistency and genuine passion for the music. These attributes have served him well. He became a great player. His musical skill came to the forefront not only as a master dance player but also a concert fiddler. It might be fair to say that a fiddler can excel in one or the other through honest effort. But to excel in both the dance and soloist traditions as Buddy MacMaster has done is unusual, even within the Cape Breton tradition.

Buddy holds the music of many early players in high esteem and explains that several select fiddlers had a direct impact. Little Jack Mac-Donald, Angus Chisholm, William (Bill) Lamey and Little Mary Mac-Donald had a major influence on his music. Musicians/composers like Dan R. MacDonald and Dan Hughie MacEachern were also very influential. Who were these idols who visited Judique and played their music at the MacMaster home? What might they have had to offer Buddy Mac-Master in his formative days as he nurtured his interest for and within the music tradition?

Jimmy MacInnis in *Eilean Cheap Breatann* and Allister MacGillivray in *The Cape Breton Fiddler* give a wonderful description of some of Buddy's idols. These fiddlers represent an excellent illustration of the music that was practised in their lifetime and Buddy was fortunate to be close enough to them to learn by listening and watching.

"Hearing my mother talk about Little Jack when I was little taught me how much she appreciated them [the fiddlers], so I came to understand that a fiddler was a pretty special person," says Buddy. "I loved the sound of the music and the sound of the fiddle."

Little Jack MacDonald (1887-1969) was born in Judique and travelled with his music early in life. In Montreal, he was inspired to learn to read music and became a serious student of the note. He applied this skill especially to the Scottish tunes he had acquired – the music compositions of Niel Gow (1727-1807), William Marshall (1748-1833) and James Scott Skinner (1843-1927). While living in Detroit, he would attend concerts by Fritz Kreisler and Jascha Heifetz – as if to study their style and technique. He applied the cuts to his music with ease. He had developed a great bow hand and especially enjoyed the pastoral airs.

Angus Chisholm (1908-1979) was born in Margaree. Initially, he had learned to play by ear without the use of the written music. He was later influenced to read music by Jimmy MacInnis of Rear Big Pond, who had acquired an understanding of classical music. MacInnis taught Chisholm to execute positioning. Chisholm, too, mastered the technique of cuttings and like Little Jack, he performed the music of the Scottish composers with precision and brilliance.

Bill Lamey (1914-1991), born in River Denys, learned to read music early in his career. He had a voracious appetite for new tunes and acquired one of the most comprehensive collections of written music for the violin and the Scottish bagpipe. Lamey mastered a technique for great bowing and impeccable cuttings in his music. He was a popular dance player and performed his music regularly throughout Cape Breton before moving to Boston, where he continued a career performing and promoting the music.

Little Mary MacDonald (1897-1983), born at MacKinnon's Brook, Mabou, mastered the Gaelic sound. Her music was embedded in the aural tradition and was representative of the Mabou Coal Mines style. She had acquired a wonderful repertoire of the traditional tunes. Applying a unique bow hand was her trademark. She often played the old tunes in the distinctive high bass. Mary MacDonald was one of Cape Breton's most noted and gifted traditional players.

Buddy's mentors were masters in the art of good fiddling and they had their own mentors from earlier generations. Yet they were clearly distinctive in the manner in which they played the fiddle. Their distinct styles were evident and consistent in any tune they rendered. There was no mistaking Chisholm for Lamey or Little Mary for Little Jack and yet their sound is distinctively Cape Breton. This was, and continues to be, imperative to the tradition. Buddy was able to appreciate the explicit style and subtle nuances of these particular fiddlers on the one hand but was also to interpret the music in a manner that would allow him to acquire his own style.

Through his bowing, Buddy accents the cuttings (triplets) in both the up and down stroke. His fingering routine is crisp and the inclusion of rapid grace notes helps to embellish the tunes in a range of melodic and rhythmical patterns. The drive and the lift in his music are the essence of his dance music. His touch renders a sweet music that evokes special feelings in his pastoral airs especially. His repertoire is varied and consists of a huge volume of music from Cape Breton and Scotland as well as Ireland. Yet Buddy's sound is identifiably Cape Breton – especially Inverness County – and, indeed, clearly demonstrates his regard for the playing of the early masters, a title that has described Buddy's place in the tradition for decades.

Buddy is an exceptionally modest person. To ask him to offer a comment about his style in music, for example, will not likely elicit any lengthy dissertation, usually no more than a few sentences. His response is even less when asked to discuss his achievements. He is a person of few words.

To describe Buddy's style is a challenge. As is the case in the music of his mentors, there are so many variables to consider. There is timing, repertoire, embellishment, positioning, tuning, tone, bowing, ornamentation, scale range, assimilation, and the written note, to name a few. The context – the dance hall, the concert, the studio – in which the fiddler performs determines style. Performing as a soloist rather than in a group of two or more also dictates style. These are all relevant when describing a fiddler's style, and they vary from fiddler to fiddler. In addition, one can add stamina, presentation, consistency and distinctiveness. Some may excel in some areas and not so much in others. In a tradition where listening is important, there is a tendency to simply play – make music. How the musician applies technique and style is important only to a person who is actually trying to learn the instrument.

Interviewing Buddy on CIGO Radio in Port Hawkesbury in July 2000, Bobby MacEachern asked him to describe his style. As if to suggest that there is not really a whole lot to his music, Buddy said, "Well, I always wanted to include brightness and liveliness ... and play sweet music ... pleasing to the ear ... and when playing some slow airs I try and give them feeling. So, I try to do those things. I don't know how well I'm doing but that's what I have in mind when I'm playing. And I try to have a good tempo, good timing. I don't like the music too fast but you can play lively without playing fast. Of course, you have to have pretty good tempo ... you know ... too draggy or slow is not good either." [He laughs.]

Bobby MacEachern wants Buddy to comment on the manner in which he includes "grace notes" in his music. Grace notes are a quick, repetitive rendering of notes that accent a musical phrase without inhibiting correct rhythm or timing. Those who have come to know and appreciate Buddy's music understand that he is an exceptional exponent of this aspect of the Cape Breton fiddling tradition. But Buddy prefers to answer MacEachern in a more general manner. He refers to the application of this skill by fiddlers other than himself.

"The ornamentation, the grace notes, in other words ... adds to the music. Of course, you can overdo that, too, you know. I think some ornamentation certainly makes the music more pleasing to listen to and ... well, different fiddlers [have a] slightly different touch and different ornamentation, and some fiddlers use very little ornamentation and yet they are good players ... They have some other feeling they put into the music, good timing, a nice touch that is pleasing to listen to ...

"Some of the players, and some of the older players, had very nimble fingers, you know, it's like handwriting. Some people naturally are better handwriters ... and it is the same with the violin. If you have the nimble fingers you can add these grace notes to the music ... it seems to come out better. Some of the better players, in the past ... I'll mention Angus Chisholm and Winston Scotty Fitzgerald and many others ... had very nimble quick fingers and so they were very popular fiddlers ... Then you have the coordination between your left and right hand – the bowing and the fingering ... some have the talent and the gift more than others.

"It [the ornamentation] gives the Gaelic flavour to the music, I think, you know. There's some debating whether the Gaelic has anything to do with Cape Breton fiddling. I believe it does, you know."

Joey Beaton has travelled extensively with Buddy for many years. In an interview with Bobby MacEachern, he said, "Well, Buddy has a very lovely style. Buddy knows when to use a long bow and also when to use a short bow ... That knowledge makes him very, very special ... He brings a lot of zest to his music. And as I watch Buddy play year after year, I cannot help but be overwhelmed by his tremendous tone and his precision timing. His tempo is just remarkable. He can adapt himself to any situation.

"If he is playing a slow air at a funeral, he'll put his proper stamp on that, in my view. If he is going to play for a stepdancer at a concert, Buddy is right there driving 'er on the strathspeys and reels. So he is an all round top-notch fiddler ...

"The slow airs are very emotional. I think Buddy tries to depict what the composer is trying to say in his composition, and Buddy puts himself in the composer's place and brings to light the emotions, whether they are sadness or happiness or whether it is a celebration of a joyous occasion or whatever ... Buddy seems to be always able to bring that out, particularly in the slow airs."

Doug MacPhee comments on Buddy's style: "He accomplished what he set out to do. He has impeccable timing. He is one of the great dance players of our time. He has a great drive in his music. He has a sweet tone and yet he has a wonderful life in his music. His intonation is dead on ... His fingering is always spot on. He just snaps them on the strings so quickly ... so effectively. He gives the note the full value ... a good solid musician. Listen to Buddy playing the marches, the strathspeys and the reels on some old tapes from the 1950s and the 1960s and listen to him today. You hear that same drive in his music. He doesn't vary. He is particular about his notes. He is a stickler for correctness but yet his music is not boring. It is filled with spontaneity. His bowing is great. He always takes the best quality from the tune – new or old. He plays those old tunes no differently now. His consistency is so obvious. He never forgets the old tunes. Dan Joe MacInnis once said to me, 'There is no new tune worth learning if it means forgetting an old tune.' I think that Buddy might agree with that, too."

Jody Stecher, in *Strings,* effectively describes Buddy's bowing and style: "Unique to Buddy is in his tone, his timing, his choice of tunes and the order in which he plays them, a rare combination of gracefulness and power, and a depth of feeling with a religious tinge not found in all fiddling ... His bowing is assertive and the music heavily accented. Using mostly single bow strokes, his bow has a force going up and down. The first beat in a measure is typically played with a down-bow, and the force of the bow on the up-bow on the offbeat gives the music tremendous lift. Accents are also produced by bowed triplets, called 'cuts' or 'cuttings,' and by a variety of left-hand ornaments, which are also used to beautify the melody and give it character."

In addition, Stecher gives a vivid account of how Buddy is so adept at the inclusion of ornamentation in his music. "MacMaster's grace notes always occur in the same bow stroke as a note decorated. They range from simply approaching a note from an open string, to lifting a higher finger to reveal the melody note, to mordents and trills, to an unusual and thrilling rocking ornament that I've heard mostly on the note G and on the E string. This is achieved by keeping the first finger behind the second, releasing some of the pressure on the second finger without actually lifting it and swiftly returning the pressure harder than before, all while rocking the hand. When the pressure is restored, the rocking becomes more rapid. Buddy's version of this universal Cape Breton-ism is very rapid with a relatively small pitch oscillation.

"Sometimes he includes a quirk in barely audible hammer thumb from the open E string before the G is sounded. He makes moderate but effective use of double stops, of drones even less but uses E, A and D unisons very freely. During these unisons the note on the open string may be raised a step and returned, while the fourth finger holds steady on the lower string. More frequently, MacMaster bows two adjacent strings, the higher of which is sounded open, the identical pitch on the lower string coming just afterwards, having arrived from a lower note and stopped by the third, second, or first finger – the fourth finger landing in its proper place and with sweet emphasis. Buddy uses vibrato as an ornament, adding colour and accents to certain selected notes. It is one of his trademark sounds and is produced quite differently from classical vibrato because Buddy bends his wrist back and presses firmly against the heel of his violin neck. A corollary of this wrist position is that the strings are contacted below the fingertips, giving the instrument a characteristic Cape Breton tone.

"Buddy grips the bow just above the frog, using primarily his thumb and his first finger; the fourth and second fingers occasionally leave the bow entirely. Buddy's sense of pitch or tonality is very striking. His C in A minor, for instance, is often higher than C natural. This and other microtonal shadings link his fiddling with the old Gaelic music and give it an edge that really makes one sit up and listen."

Stecher addresses Buddy's strong "intuitive" abilities as a musician and performer. "MacMaster neither composes nor improvises. His creative abilities go into expression creating melodies, a skill involving intuitive editorial logic, for which he is justly famous. At informal sessions or especially at a dance, Buddy MacMaster's musical abilities come into full bloom. Before he hits his stride, he will typically play each tune twice before moving on to the next. Like all players in this tradition and in any one medley Buddy will keep to one key or around one tonal centre, for instance A. This allows the music to build in intensity and depth, and also creates a light trance in the listener, dancer, and player that would be broken by key change."

It is this skill set that Buddy would take on the road to a greater audience of folk and fiddle enthusiasts beginning in the early 1970s.

Dan R. MacDonald (1911-1976) of Judique South and Dan Hughie MacEachern (1914-1996) of Queensville were wonderful fiddlers held in high esteem by Buddy. The feeling and respect were mutual. In Cape Breton, the greatest contribution from Dan R. and Dan Hughie is the repository of tunes they composed for local fiddlers, tunes that are now commonplace among the musicians who play Celtic music worldwide. Between the two of them, they may have composed as many as three thousand tunes, many of which have been published. Dan Hughie was a master at the note – reading music. He was also a wonderful composer and player.

In his recollection about learning to read music, Buddy often refers to

Dan Hughie MacEachern. "Dan Hughie was a very good friend of mine ... through the years ... since I was a young boy," says Buddy. "The first time I met Dan Hughie was at a picnic in Judique and as far as I can remember he was nineteen years old [in 1933]. He was playing on the stage ... I think I was just starting to play at that time ... and I was very interested in the fiddle and in his playing ... then after that he used to come over to Judique to visit ... My sister [Kathleen] would play the piano ... There were good listeners in our home. Dan Hughie would start playing around eight o'clock and play straight through till all hours of the night. He had more tunes than anybody I ever heard. He never ran out of tunes ... difficult to play [and] in all keys. So through the years I knew Dan Hughie well ... He'd play sweet music . . .

"He also was a great composer – composed many, many tunes: jigs, strathspeys, reels, hornpipes and marches. He wrote 'The Trip to Mabou Ridge,' which is a terrific march and which is still played a lot. It was composed in 1938. There is a little story in back of that [there are several versions]. He was working at Port Hood at the time. They hired him to play for a dance in Mabou Ridge ... Angus Hughie MacEachern came down with him on the train ... There was a big snowstorm ... Angus Rankin from Mabou Ridge met them at the railway station train. [He] took them up to Mabou Ridge in time for the dance. When they got to the hall they couldn't get the door opened ... All the snow [had] drifted around. They had to go in through the window ... it was quite a memorable trip. Buddy recalls that Dan Hughie was purported to have said, 'I'm going to make a tune for this trip.'

"[Dan Hughie] liked the old style of playing ... His tunes resembled tunes that were composed in Scotland. Of course, he had his own style as well but he composed great tunes ... all different keys, E Minor, C, B Flat, B Minor. He composed some tunes for the high bass ... He played a lot of that high bass himself. [His tunes] were great for dancing ... the jigs were excellent for dancing ... he composed a lot of great reels – 'The Snow Plow Reel,' the 'Boisdale Reel.'"

Buddy explains that when Dan Hughie visited the MacMaster homestead, he would encourage Buddy to not only play but also to learn the note. Buddy's initial reluctance for reading music was not unusual. Most young fiddlers in the tradition now and in the past are a bit reluctant to hit the note – the books – too early. Some wait for as many as eight to ten years of playing by ear before learning to read the music. Some never read and still become excellent fiddlers.

"I was too young and did not have the interest in the note reading then. I just wanted to play the fiddle. So, I did not take advantage of Dan Hughie's interest in having me reading the note. I recall that whenever I'd see Dan Hughie at the local store I'd tend to shy away from him for fear that he might ask how the note reading was going. [He laughs.] I was just a young fellow at the time.

"But I knew that I wanted to play correctly. I knew that was important. Before being able to read, I was certain to learn my tunes from the fiddlers who were good at reading. That way I would learn the tunes as correct as possible. Now I heard Hughie T. MacDonnell play a lot. He was not a reader but he had a good ear. He would hang around fiddlers like Little Jack, and Little Jack could read [music]. All the fiddlers would visit Hughie T.'s house and they could read the note. But Hughie T. always encouraged me to learn to read.

"Bill Lamey was a great influence [on Buddy's interest to read the note]. Bill was into the books even at a young age. He made a few visits and he would play the old tunes and he played so correct." [Buddy takes a moment to whistle a few of the old tunes Bill once played and that he had learned from Bill.]

Buddy was very perceptive as a young fiddler. He learned a great deal about the music from these wonderful fiddlers. He also learned a lot about wit and diplomacy. He shared a story about being in the company of two fiddlers on a particular occasion, whose music he always enjoyed immensely. He would have been about fifteen, he recalls. One of the fiddlers was Little Jack MacDonald and the other was Gordon MacQuarrie. Both were exceptional players and were known as such in the community.

"Little Jack was there and they got him up to play. And he had quite a name. He was a good player. Gordon was there, too. And this guy who was standing beside Gordon asked, 'Is he [Little Jack] any good, Gordon?' And Gordon looked at the guy and said, 'Well, aren't you listening to him yourself?'" [Buddy laughs.]

In 1948, while preparing to work in Antigonish, Buddy was directed to go to a boarding house in the town. When he entered his room upstairs, he noticed a young man fast asleep in the bed across the room; the young man awoke and they began a conversation. He was John Dan Delaney, a young Inverness musician who played the piano and saxophone. Based on Delaney's stories, Buddy realized this fellow was well-connected to the music scene in the Antigonish area. Buddy explained to Delaney that he played the violin.

"This guy was an army guy. He was a good friend of Rod Chisholm ... [who] was one of his teachers. Rod was at the university then. [Delaney] knew where all the parties were. I'd work until midnight as I was on the four to twelve shift. Someone would meet me after work and take me to the parties. Delaney would be there, too. I would play all night, as I did not have to be at work again until four p.m. the next day. It was quite a racket, you know."

In time, Delaney advised him that he should consider visiting Mildred Leadbeater, who was living in Antigonish at the time. Buddy explains, "She was from Glace Bay. She was a MacEachern. I think ... Leadbeaters were good musicians, too. That's why [Delaney] took me over there."

She was a proficient pianist and had her own radio program on CJFX. Delaney suggested to Buddy that he might learn to read music from her. So he took the advice and introduced himself to Leadbeater. She gave an illustration of the notes on a single piece of paper; it was the tune "Irish Washerwoman." Buddy began to tinker with that for a bit.

Later, Buddy made his way to the Celtic music store on Main Street, where he purchased an instructional book to help him master the note. The book provided a variety of illustrations. Buddy explains that it showed how to hold the violin and the bow "properly." "I looked pretty professional for awhile," he laughs. "But then I settled back into my own way of doing things." Buddy explains that within no time he went back to the same music store and purchased *The Scottish Violinist* by J. Scott Skinner, which was his first music book.

Shortly thereafter, Buddy met Angus D.D. MacDonald, who owned a clothing store in Antigonish. "He asked me if I would like to play a program on the radio to advertise his store. I thought it was a great idea. So I decided that I would play a couple of tunes from the Skinner book. All went well. That was my first performance on radio. [He laughs.] My knees were knocking the whole time. That was in 1948. I believe I went a second time as well. I believe Bessie MacDonald accompanied me. She had been playing piano for a lot of the fiddlers at the time."

Over the years, Buddy compiled a number of excellent rare music books. In his collection are originals and a number of reissues. He had written to music stores in Scotland as others had been doing. John Grant Music Store in Glasgow was a favourite. "I was visiting Scotland in the early 1970s. I went to that Grant's store. He told me to go upstairs to see what was there. I came across some good Gow stuff."

Later in the 1970s, Buddy's uncle, Charlie MacMaster, put him in touch with a gentleman in Boston who had an excellent collection of music books. Subsequently, Buddy was able to acquire some of these rare books. Buddy explains, "I recall I got the Marshall Collection and a Gow book which was seven collections in one. It was a great book, you know. I paid a few hundred dollars for the works. Dan R. and I agreed it was a good deal."

As if to come full circle, countless tunes have been composed for Buddy MacMaster and many appear in a wide range of publications. Tradition bearers regard this as a deep mark of respect. For a person to have had a tune composed in his or her honour is special. Many outstanding composers – Dan Hughie MacEachern, Donald Angus Beaton, Kinnon Beaton, Joey Beaton, John Campbell, and Jerry Holland, to name a few – wrote tunes to honour Buddy MacMaster – marches, strathspeys, reels, jigs, slow airs and hornpipes. The musical compositions of these gifted composers are respected worldwide.

Among dance music enthusiasts, Buddy MacMaster is often referred to as the "King of the Jig." Rev. Eugene Morris, a celebrated dancer from Inverness County, states, "One of the finest tunes written for Buddy in recent years is Kinnon Beaton's composition 'The Order of Canada Jig' to commemorate Buddy being awarded the Order of Canada in 2000."

But the composer/fiddler with whom Buddy had best developed that

Buddy enjoying a break between tunes with his daughter, Mary Elizabeth, at the piano.

Performing at the Dan Hughie MacEachern Tribute Ceilidh, hosted by Cape Breton University, in 1980. Left to right: Father Francis Cameron, Boisdale; Buddy; Carl MacKenzie, Sydney Forks; Father Angus Morris, Mabou; and Doug MacPhee, New Waterford, at the piano.

John Morris Rankin and Buddy prepare for Buddy's first solo recording, *Judique on the Floor*, in 1989.

Buddy with his sister Genevieve Whalen, who also accompanied him on piano. (Judique Hall, 2004)

Buddy with his two sisters who often accompanied him on piano: Lorraine MacDonnell (left) and Betty Beaton at Glencoe Mills, 1990.

special friendship and respect felt among certain fiddlers was Dan R. MacDonald (1911-1976). Celebrated as one of the greatest composers of the twentieth century, Dan R.'s music is played wherever Celtic music is performed. Dan R. and Buddy enjoyed a special relationship.

John Donald Cameron explains the respect that his uncle Dan R. MacDonald and Buddy MacMaster had for one another. "Buddy was good to Dan R. ... [Dan R.] gave him a lot of music. I'd say that he gave music to Buddy [to play] before he gave it to anybody else ... because he knew Buddy would be playing at dances ... and getting the tunes out [to other fiddlers] to play." [Apart from a few selections that were published in 1940, Dan R.'s music was not published in any significant volume until after his passing.]

One of Dan R.'s most famous tunes is the beautiful "Glencoe March." John Donald Cameron explains the march was composed as a dedication to Buddy. John Donald remarks that the famous Scottish composer James Scott Skinner would compose a tune and give it a title, but he would make a notation in brackets after the title noting the person to whom the tune was dedicated. "Dan R. didn't do that ... but some of us knew to whom he was dedicating the tunes. He composed a jig for me ... the 'Newfoundland Jig' ... I was working in Newfoundland at the time.

"[Dan R.] went to a dance at Glencoe in 1970 ... Buddy was playing, of course ... and he enjoyed it, of course, very much ... so the next day he decided ... this tune came to his mind and he said he was going to compose something reminiscent of the night before. So, he composed the 'Glencoe March' ... He wrote it out and gave it to Buddy ... and Buddy was the first to play it. Of course, it is probably Dan R.'s most famous tune [he composed over 2,000] other than 'Heather Hill' and 'Trip to Windsor.' It ranks up there. It is interesting as it was composed just six years before he died. It was dedicated to Buddy and his name should be there in brackets [as Scott Skinner would do]. He also composed another tune for Buddy – a reel – 'Buddy's Favorite.'"

John Donald tells a story that took place in 1966 when he and Dan R. were visiting Buddy. Along the way in the car, Dan R. told John Donald that he was going to play a new tune for Buddy. In Buddy's kitchen, Dan R. played his composition "Moxham Castle." As soon as Buddy observed that it would be a good stepdancing tune, Dan R. said, "You can have it."

John Donald notes that it is hard to introduce new tunes for step-dancing as the dancers like certain ones. But John Donald believes that Buddy's addition of it to his repertoire made "Moxham Castle" a popular choice for step-dancing, as it is now commonly heard.

Buddy has acquired a respect for the written music throughout his lifetime. His performances and music collections speak volumes about that. He came to know the written music in a special way. Buddy received tunes from published collections but just as often the music came informally on single sheets of paper, from friends and strangers. Most of these tunes were presented in a manner that would allow Buddy to discern the music, but there were bits of tunes that were often presented in very rough form. In addition, Buddy respected the place of the composer and always wanted to know from whence the tune came. Why was it written? To whom might it be dedicated? Buddy wants to know more than a melody. He holds steadfastly to this.

John Donald Cameron explains. "He appreciates what the music is about. He wants to know the background of the music. I don't think Buddy will play a tune, even to this day, unless he knows where it came from. If someone gives him a tune out of the blue he won't play it. And I like that. I agree with that. I feel that same way ... [Buddy] likes to know what it is about or where it came from ... I think that's a strong plus ... He may not always know the title ... and that is not as important ... but it is more important to know where it came from and who wrote it ... [know] what book it came from ... something about it ... Fiddle tunes are about people, about the area ... There're about our people ... the same way Gaelic songs are written ... It all relates."

The information that Buddy acquires about the tunes as a result of his own questions and research is something that he values, and he is always willing to share that detail with anyone who is interested. But commenting on the detail at a public performance was, and is not, an integral aspect of his performance. In that context, playing the music for the listening enjoyment of the audience is the main objective. The point is Buddy would not take it upon himself to present a dissertation about the music's background at his performances. On the contrary, he has always presented a very quiet demeanour on stage. It is fair to say that in more recent years he has been called upon to comment more in the public setting than in the past, due in large part to his participation in conducting workshops for music enthusiasts from outside the tradition. The knowledge Buddy acquired about a tune, the background, was for him personally. It is a mark of respect for the tune and the composer. Buddy accepts that for most members in a general audience that "a fiddle tune is a fiddle tune." This, of course, is not the case for Buddy MacMaster.

Hit the Road

Between 1939 and 1969, Buddy MacMaster's performance venues were primarily wherever Cape Bretoners would gather – in Cape Breton or among Cape Bretoners who had settled in "the Boston States." This routine kept him on the go at a hectic pace. It also contained Buddy to audiences who were comfortable with and knowledgeable about the music and the various settings where the music was played.

Buddy performed at many of the old-time outdoor concerts and picnics over the years. In rural Cape Breton, there has been a longstanding tradition of Sunday concerts, hosted primarily by Catholic parishes to raise money for church and community-related activities. The amenities were few. Nevertheless, they attracted thousands who would sit for hours on the rough wooden benches or, alternatively, patrons would respond to the call to take along lawn chairs. Either way, the event began in the early afternoon and lasted until early evening, and those in attendance had both a critical eye and a sharp ear. Performers included young and old from the best of the island's music scene. Of course, the host community would showcase many of the acts from that community. But one performer who seemed to attend regardless of which community was hosting was Buddy MacMaster.

"Well, I like going to those concerts," says Buddy. "You meet other fiddlers who you may not have seen for a long time ... and they help make money for the community to do some nice things. I like them all ... I think the people enjoy them, too. They always seem to get nice crowds ... Some are more popular than others but they are all nice. I played at most of them, I guess, over the years. I guess they are changing, too, these days ... There is so much going on now with the music ... it is hard to keep up with it all. A fellow could be going all day and all night." [He laughs.]

Historically, these concerts took place in a large farm field. A wide-open stage usually built by local volunteer carpenters was designed to hold for the day. They were equipped with a modest sound system to showcase the musicians. These concerts served as a mainstay for the music. The routine introduced popular fiddlers, pipers, dancers and Gaelic singers who were featured primarily as soloists. They were representative of the grassroots music tradition and these venues often served to nurture many of the Celtic music stars who today travel the world – Natalie MacMaster, Andrea Beaton, Howie MacDonald, Ashley MacIsaac, Mairi Rankin and Mac Morin.

Crowds gathered from across Cape Breton in the summer months as the venue played host to visitors whether they were native Cape Bretoners on holiday and visiting family or the typical American tourist looking for an experience in the Cape Breton music tradition. Buddy was and is a popular figure at these concerts and not to include him as part of the litany of performers was certain to disappoint many. The setting was a dynamic catalyst for musicians "behind the rugged wire fence" to meet and share tunes and stories, and for members of the audience to become reacquainted with extended family and friends from all walks of life. The atmosphere was more like an annual homecoming. Small rural communities like Broad Cove (Inverness County), Iona (Victoria County) and Big Pond (Cape Breton County) have been significant builders of this tradition. Broad Cove is often referred to as the "granddaddy" of them all as it was initiated in 1957 and set the standard for the many other sites to follow. Buddy appeared at the first Broad Cove concert just as he did at the fiftieth anniversary concert, which took place in July 2006. He missed very few in between and when that did happen, it would only have been because he was away performing at some festival outside Cape Breton.

Tila Lamb is from Boston. She has deep Cape Breton roots and has acquired a fond interest in the music. She visits often. "I attended my first Broad Cove concert [in 2006]. And I heard Buddy MacMaster. He is a class act. I heard him in Boston, of course. I so enjoyed the wonderful atmosphere at Broad Cove. I was able to see people from the States as well as Cape Breton. There was chatting among many people. You could almost feel the excitement. At one point that afternoon while we were on the field, we heard them announce that Buddy would be playing at the concert. Later, it was announced that it was now Buddy's turn. There was an amazing silence all around the field. Everyone wanted to hear him play. There were thousands of people just listening to this wonderful player. It was like there was this great sense of awe that fell over everyone."

Buddy also made regular appearances at the Nova Scotia Highland Village Day concert. That program began in 1962 and continues as an integral feature of the festive summer activities developed at the Highland Village Museum in Iona. The Big Pond annual concert celebrated a twenty-fifth anniversary program in 1989 with week-long festivities. Buddy was among the special guest artists who appeared at that program and at many before and since. As with the Broad Cove gatherings, there were very few Big Pond concerts that Buddy missed over the years.

Jack MacNeil is a co-founder of the Big Pond Summer Concert series, which he served from 1964 to 1992. He makes the following comment: "For the most part, my contact with Buddy MacMaster was through the Big Pond concert. High on the wish list of the concert committee each year – not far below good weather – was the presence of Buddy Mac-Master. And when weather was pleasant as we came to opening time and promised to remain so, and someone had leaned in a backstage doorway to give the word 'Buddy is on the field!' all was right with the world and we were on a roll.

"He is, of course, one of our greatest and best loved musicians, and a great ambassador for our music, but when he comes to mind, I usually think of the man before I think of the musician. For me, he is first and foremost a fine gentleman of the old school, the Cape Bretoner at his best, for whom courtesy and civility and respect still matter, even though

Buddy performing at the Big Pond
Summer Festival in 1989.

Part of the audience at the Big Pond Summer Festival in 1989 – a typical concert setting
in rural Cape Breton at the time in communities like Big Pond, Broad Cove and Iona.

CBC *Ceilidh* fiddlers, mid-1970s. Left to right: Buddy MacMaster, Winnie Chafe, John Campbell and Sandy MacIntyre.

Visiting Scotland in 1984 with the Cape Breton Symphony and guests: Graham Townsend, a Canadian fiddler, Buddy and John Donald Cameron, fiddler and a founding member of the Cape Breton Symphony.

they now at times seem a bit out of fashion. Being around Buddy makes us better people."

By the 1970s, a greater interest in the folk music genre in general had developed worldwide. This opened new playing, new venues and new audiences to engage. Buddy would strive to present his music in the way he always had but often he would meet challenges in the studio, in concert tours and in television.

An important feature of the local routine or tradition for Buddy was that he would determine the tunes and the order in which he would play them. Group fiddling in a house session or in a public concert was also very much part of the tradition. In a group performance, the soloists would be highlighted first. This is an important feature in the Cape Breton music tradition. In this setting, three or more fiddlers would convene for some serious music. In addition, musicians would share stories about the music – about tunes, composers, collections and so on. Sessions could go for several hours in private homes. This is an important element in the learning process. These meetings would provide the opportunity for the listener to learn. To bring closure to a session, fiddlers would rally to play in unison, rendering a full range of music over a significant period of time. The dynamics in this setting are fascinating to experience.

A spontaneous group performance would often close out a public concert – the finale – that would feature as many as fifteen fiddlers. In the group performances, one fiddler would be selected to lead the others in the medley of tunes played. Usually, the standard tunes would prevail; following the leader was, therefore, easy for most. The format became an entertaining feature at some gatherings but not central to the program.

These fiddlers also appeared as soloists, first and foremost, with solo dancers, pipers and singers. To be asked to perform at a concert and not be given a solo spot would be highly unusual. The place of the individual performance was the dominant feature and remains so today. The group style has become much more prevalent today with, in part, the arrival of the 1973 Cape Breton Fiddlers Festival.

The Cape Breton Fiddlers' Association is a very active entity. The organization hosts a series of activities for the local fiddlers, the most significant of which is the annual Festival of Cape Breton Fiddling, now staged at the Gaelic College of Arts and Crafts, St. Ann's, Victoria County. In addition, invitations to participate at festivals elsewhere in Canada are sometimes considered, such as the Rollo Bay Festival in Prince Edward Island, the Royal Nova Scotia International Tattoo and the Glengarry Games in Ontario. These are special attractions for the Cape Breton members, who also visited festivals in British Columbia and New Brunswick. This fellowship among the Cape Breton fiddlers through the association is great for the music. The fiddlers gather monthly in the fall and winter to practise the tunes. Buddy MacMaster, when scheduling permits, has been very loyal to this program and his participation has helped the association immensely.

Betty Matheson, who manages the arrangements for the association, says about Buddy's participation, "Buddy's presence is a great support in our efforts to promote the music. He is highly respected by all the fiddlers, not only in Cape Breton but wherever Scottish fiddle music is played. He is so well-liked and appreciated ... A highlight on our trips when Buddy can be with us is to have him entertain on some of the long bus rides ... Just picture, if you can, a comfortable bus with fifty or sixty fiddlers on board winding along the highway ... passengers obviously love the music ... and everyone is relaxed. Buddy takes out his fiddle and begins to play ... for hours as we pass through the small towns and villages in Ontario or New Brunswick or Nova Scotia ... Buddy is performing for his favourite audience – a group of Cape Breton fiddlers. [She laughs.] ... These travels are very fond memories among our fiddlers."

There were greater challenges at other venues, however, especially in CBC's TV program *Ceilidh*, which Buddy joined in 1972. *Ceilidh* was produced in Halifax and hosted by well-known entertainer John Allan Cameron. There were challenges to Buddy's playing style again in 1979 when he joined the Cape Breton Symphony, which was founded in 1974.

John Allan was related to Buddy through the MacDonalds. But apart from the family link, John Allan and Buddy respected each other's music. In fact, Buddy was very encouraging of the Cameron family's interest in the music. The Cameron boys (John Allan and John Donald), in their younger days, looked up to Buddy as a role model. John Allan would disappear from his home at Glencoe Station for hours, only to be discovered at the MacMaster household playing guitar and accompanying Buddy.

One aspect of the programmed and rehearsed medleys for TV was the ever so seemingly insignificant and subtle use of the pianist to introduce the medleys. This was a minor detail but it took many fiddlers some time getting used to it. Simply put, the pianist would begin with a few notes or a bar to get the music started. Then the fiddlers were to enter at the same time and on the same note together. This was different, but important to the slick and more polished sound expected by TV standards. In the traditional manner, the fiddlers were accustomed to starting and anyone else participating, piano or otherwise, had to jump in.

Another dominant and more obvious feature for the fiddlers on *Ceilidh* was the regular group performances. In this context, it was important that the fiddlers organize more as a unit. This became the norm for the TV show. John Allan often consulted his brother John Donald, a fiddler, for ideas and direction, although John Donald was not on the program as a performer. John Donald recognized that the unit was important, even though it was somewhat against the conventional way of performing in the Cape Breton tradition. Perhaps the nearest template in living memory would have been the performances of the Five MacDonald Fiddlers, not all related to each other, but all of whom had deep Cape Breton roots. The MacDonald Fiddlers were together in the Detroit/Windsor area in the 1960s, and they released a series of commercial recordings. A few infrequent concert appearances took place.

Thus, the CBC production *Ceilidh* required some patience and good leadership to format the unit. John Donald's recollections about the CBC production on that point are that Buddy took the initiative and encouraged the initial six *Ceilidh* fiddlers to work at the concept. Subsequently, other fiddlers became adept at taking on this role. The entire production was centred around scores that were standardized and prepared for all the musicians who were on the set. Instruments such as base, drum, accordion and others were all assembled at different times to participate in the weekly production. For Buddy and other fiddlers, this was a bit of a step away from the Cape Breton tradition, although it was well-known in Scottish bands, and had also proven to be successful with Winston

"Scotty" Fitzgerald and his Sydney-based orchestra. He incorporated the style on live radio and TV in Sydney in the 1950s and at some of his dances that were part of his circuit at that time. That style of presentation served Scotty effectively but was still not a feature within the tradition generally. The ideas of compatibility, harmony, consistency and time marks for the CBC production were important. This was a relatively new feature for most of the Cape Breton fiddlers, however, to endorse. But all went forward smoothly.

Doug MacPhee explains, "I played with Buddy for five years on *Ceilidh* in Halifax. At that time, we would go to Halifax and tape thirteen shows over a four-week period. We'd often drive up together. I'd meet him in Troy as I would leave my car at Jeanette and A.J.'s [Beaton] — just down the road from Buddy's home and we'd go together from there. We'd tape thirty-nine shows a year using that format. It was very busy. That CBC stuff was somewhat grueling, you know. And Buddy was there through thick and thin.

"But he remained true to his musical roots. He'd do all the things that were asked of him to accommodate the different interests in playing styles and dancing. But he would leave all that behind when the gig was finished. His music is so rooted. He couldn't go against the grain. For him to change his style or his music would be going backwards – not forward. He kept the old music alive and well."

By 1974, John Allan Cameron had left CBC for CTV. There, he began a partnership with Bobby Brown, a well-known pianist from Scotland who had moved to Canada in the 1950s. In fact, CTV presented the new *John Allan Cameron Show* from a station in Montreal. Bobby's musical style and presentation were very much embedded in the unit, group or band approach. He was accustomed to providing the musical leadership that would help a group function well together. In 1974, John Allan and Bobby formed the Cape Breton Symphony. The music of the Cape Breton fiddler was an important feature of the group. According to John Donald Cameron, a seasoned group of fiddlers was assembled, which included Angus Chisholm, Wilfred Gillis, Jerry Holland and John Donald himself. The approach to presenting the spontaneity in the music changed somewhat, all in the interest of professionalism and the need for the music to appeal to a wider audience and musicianship as well. As Graham

Townsend, a down-east style fiddler, and the Ottawa Dancers were often featured on the show, the Cape Breton fiddlers had to adjust their style when playing in group performances. John Donald Cameron, who had a significant role in advising John Allan, knew that the Cape Breton audiences were the most critical of the Symphony's format. The Symphony understood that, and they understood why. But they moved on to international popularity in any event.

Shows were prepared well in advance. John Donald Cameron explains how this was applied to all fiddlers initially and subsequently to Buddy. "We were given a book with all the tunes – the whole repertoire that we had. We told the fiddlers what we were going to play and to practise those certain ones. If there was anything new, the music was sent to them ... a couple of days before a performance. Then we all got together and rehearsed ... to have an idea of what we were supposed to be doing. It came together that way."

In the early stages of the Symphony's development, Buddy was still with *Ceilidh*, but CBC cancelled it within a few years as it was subject to the usual reviews and cuts. In 1979, Buddy joined the Symphony while they were on a tour in British Columbia. Of all the tours given by the Symphony, members feel that the best were the ones that took place in Scotland. But the group appeared in many parts of Canada and the U.S. and remained active until 2003. Over the years, several fiddlers, including Sandy MacIntyre and Jerry Pezzareallo, were given the honour to perform with the group.

Buddy's experience at CBC and his dedication to the Cape Breton Fiddlers' Association's monthly ceilidh had him very comfortable with the unit performance concept and he joined the Symphony's well-oiled musicians easily and gracefully. The need to prepare and then work from a form of script was as important for the professional image of the Cape Breton Symphony as it was for CBC.

John Donald describes Buddy's effort to accommodate the Symphony's style. "He worked at the tunes as scored by the musical director so that he would conform to all the music of all the musicians. The other fiddlers especially had the utmost respect for Buddy in this regard. They fully understood his tradition and that some of the tunes that he had played all his life one way were now to be played somewhat differently while with the Symphony. It was appreciated that he was so willing to work with the Symphony. One feature that was particularly appealing with the inclusion of Buddy to the cast was his wonderful timing and his use of crisp notes. He gave a great lift to the music.

"Buddy was a part of that but it did not come easily. He could not carry out any acting. He is so honest. He isn't an actor. What you see is what you get."

Doug MacPhee elaborates, "He puts the best foot forward all the time. There is no put-on with Buddy. He is always so sincere. He has it all. He has his music, but he has everything to go with it. He is a well-rounded man."

The Cape Breton Symphony also held Buddy's solo abilities in high regard. Although solo numbers were not always part of the program, there were often provisions made for Buddy to do one. John Donald explains.

"We always had Buddy do a solo because we knew there would be Cape Bretoners in the audience. [Bobby Brown asked,] 'Can you imagine us playing and Buddy with us and some Cape Bretoners in the audience and him not doing a solo?' [I replied,] 'No!' He should do one and he'll do it the way he does it down there. Let him pick out the tunes ... and that's what he did. And it always went over well. Buddy filled in that Cape Breton niche – this is what you are going to hear if you go to Cape Breton. He had that – he carried it off very well with poise and style, never showing any sense of nervousness ... His spot on the show was always early – the first half – which is not a good spot [because] the audience isn't worked up ... They're not into the thing yet ... but he never complained ... What he did was a positive thing [and] it went over so well.

"He's going to play [the music] ... the way it represents more fully the way it's played here [in Cape Breton] ... In concert tours ... you start going into too much of that commercialism ... [But] you have to bend the rules a little bit to make it more entertaining to a wider variety of audience ... But Buddy ... he might play in some other part of Canada or overseas the same as he would in the Judique hall or in Mabou ... In his case, if that's what they like, well, that's great."

In addition to his musicianship, Buddy's personal character added to the fun and enjoyment within the Cape Breton Symphony. Because he was so willing to participate in a good laugh, Buddy added to this fellowship. On one occasion, the cast decided to play a practical joke on Buddy while on stage and before a live audience. It shows the confidence and trust the group had in Buddy. The practical joke developed as planned but it allowed Buddy to have the final laugh, however.

John Donald tells the story. "One time in New Waterford, we had a sound check in the afternoon. Buddy missed it because he was working [at CN]. So, we all decided we'd play a trick on him [that night] when we are on stage and see what he will do. So, we were all lined up across the stage after one of the numbers. Then Bobby Brown came up with his [usual] comedy routine and then he said something about 'These fellows [the fiddlers] think they're getting paid for playing with me tonight. But they're not getting paid for tonight.' Of course, at that point we had made up that we were all going to walk off the stage. [At the mention of not getting paid] everybody [would walk] ... and Buddy would not know anything about it ... [Bobby makes his announcement and the fiddlers yelled as if surprised,] 'What?' We all said ... and, of course, walked off the stage. Buddy looked around ... what the hell is happening here? He didn't say a word. There was laughter. The audience laughed but everything got silent again. Buddy turned to Bobby and said [into the microphone], 'I'll play with you, Bobby.' [John Donald gives a good laugh.] So it didn't throw [Buddy] one bit. [He] was great. It was better than what we did."

The Cape Breton Symphony's and CBC's schedules, however, were added functions for Buddy. He did not relinquish his individual talent as an excellent soloist in his own right, playing in his own style and at the usual venues that he had known all his life. In fact, the public at home and abroad were even more demanding of Buddy's music and presence. They wanted him beyond the usual Cape Breton setting and wherever his time and travel would permit. In these instances, he remained loyal to his tradition and his style.

Many appearances in Cape Breton in an earlier era had already prepared Buddy for this demand. His reputation as a class performer was well established long before CBC's *Ceilidh* and Cape Breton Symphony. Doug MacPhee explains, "Back in the '50s, when I was still very young, I would hear Buddy MacMaster over CJFX radio. He would play a lot there, especially during the Antigonish Highland Games. And Genevieve, his sister, was playing with him often at that time. They were young ... and [had] lots of energy in their music. It was such a treat to listen to them. Buddy would hold my attention. Everything was so rich and so fresh and Genevieve's music was every bit like Buddy's. They were complementing each other so well. It was marvelous to hear the tunes that Buddy would be playing – book tunes – slow airs and the full range that was so much a feature in his repertoire ... and still is, of course.

"Buddy would draw you to him. He would make you sit up and take notice. Even if one were not to know the music, his stage presence was quite remarkable. He has that about him. There is a sense of magic about Buddy MacMaster. When listening to Buddy over the years regardless of his age, as a younger fiddler or later, you knew you were listening to a great musician. He always held the Gaelic sound but his was new and fresh. And you know Buddy MacMaster's music when you hear it.

"I recall Ann Terry [MacLellan] making a remark on her morning radio program at CJCB Sydney about a Scottish concert she had attended in the late '50s. And she would have such a way with words. She was gifted in her own right. I believe the concert had been organized by Father Hugh A. [MacDonald]. I believe his choir was in the concert, too. Now at that time, Ann Terry liked the music but perhaps she did not fully understand our music too much.

"Anyway, two of the guests for that concert were Buddy MacMaster and his sister Genevieve. Well, you should have heard Ann Terry on radio going on about Buddy's performance. She talked about how distinguished he was and how well-dressed he was. She described him and Genevieve being first class. She described his music as just heaven-like. I remember her words clearly. And certainly it may have been the first time she heard Buddy perform live but she was some impressed with Buddy and his sound ... his tone."

Doug adds, "He is just a great guy to be around. He is always so pleasant and always ready for a good story to make you laugh. Anytime that I'd talk with Buddy on the telephone or if we'd meet at some gathering, it was just a wonderful feeling. You know you are going to be feeling happy for having spent some time with Buddy. For me, it was always an honour to be in his company.

"I really got to know Buddy well from all the travelling we did. Over the years, we played a lot together. We played at a number of festivals in Canada and the U.S. We were to Winnipeg, Chicago, Boston and West Virginia. We often made more than one visit to these places. I was with him in Scotland, too. We are very good friends.

"I recall our visit to Calgary. We were being hosted by the young Calgary fiddlers. That was in the mid-1990s. The event was a concert and dance and took place in a school gym. In fact, it had been organized by a New Waterford native. He was vice-principal at the school. It was a great trip. He took us to Lake Louise and to Banff for a little tour. There was a very nice crowd over the weekend and they were so thrilled to see Buddy. The young fiddlers had come to know his music through their visit to Cape Breton just a couple of years earlier. You could hear a pin drop in the concert when he was playing. And the kids never missed a note. Everyone in the audience wanted to meet Buddy and say hello and shake his hand. He is one of the finest gentlemen on this earth."

The Mentor

The idea of teaching Cape Breton style fiddling in the institutional sense is a fairly recent development. John MacDougall, a fiddler/composer, was one of the most influential initially. He began teaching regular classes in Inverness County in 1972. John's program was initiated by the Cape Breton Fiddlers' Association. Other fiddlers followed – notably, Dan Joe MacInnis with a program in 1974 at Cape Breton University, which was subsequently attended by Sandy MacInnis and then later by Winnie Chafe. At the same time, Stan Chapman in Antigonish and, later, Jackie Dunn in Inverness County initiated significant developments in teaching. Other popular fiddlers like Al Bennett, Kyle MacNeil and again Stan Chapman began classes in Sydney Mines and Sydney. Since the 1980s, however, several public institutions are now involved in offering fiddle classes. Except for John MacDougall, Dan Joe MacInnis and Sandy MacInnis, most of the instructors of the past had some formal musical instruction. Accordingly, a level of methodology in teaching Cape Breton fiddle began to develop and always with some animated discussion on the process of "teaching." Cape Breton University now offers performance-based credit courses in Celtic fiddle.

Buddy would not introduce himself as a teacher in the institutional or conventional sense. However, he can be seen as an effective mentor. In this context, his greatest asset is most likely that he has made himself so available through countless performances for many to see and to hear. He often explains that he has always found it difficult to say no to anyone who asks him to perform at a function – weddings, funerals, house sessions, and the usual dance and concert scene. He has always been a very public figure with his music, but he was able to find a way to say no to setting up a regular class for students to learn from him.

He expresses his philosophy towards teaching: "Listen to a lot of other players. Watch how they use the bow and their fingers. Learn a lot of tricks, the embellishments and decorations different fiddlers use. Try to play [often] and have the tunes as correct as you can. Practise is very important."

Still, Buddy would find himself being called upon to instruct at workshops. He was asked to visit schools of fiddling and music in Britain, the United States and Canada. He travelled extensively throughout the 1980s and 1990s to perform and to give workshops. He was now very much in demand by musicians and dancers who were new to Cape Breton music. He was finding it increasingly difficult to play only. The audiences wanted even more of this man's knowledge and talent. As always, he would give his best, delivering workshops at the Valley of the Moon Scottish Fiddling School in California; at the Augusta Heritage Center in Elkins, West Virginia; at Boston College and Harvard University in Massachusetts; and at Sabhal Mòr Ostaig, Isle of Skye, Scotland. These are some of the sites he visited regularly.

Buddy's concern about entering the classroom setting is well-founded. Music educator Virginia Garrison began an important academic study in the late 1970s, culminating in the mid-1980s in a doctorate degree from the University of Wisconsin. She did an analysis on the learning and teaching process among some Cape Breton fiddlers. Garrison spent considerable time with Buddy and her findings from those discussions helped shape her understanding of the learning process that was so integral to Buddy in his formative years.

She quotes Buddy: "I think you're expressing a personality in your music, eh. You put feeling into it. It's just like handwriting – everybody has different handwriting – or the old telegraph key. I was a telegrapher and you could tell each telegrapher just from his hand sending. And they say a musical person made a better telegrapher ... Each individual has his way of expressing."

Garrison further explains the roles of learners and teachers: "The traditional transmission process in folk music is a successful process. Time has been the measure of its success. The teaching and the learning practices and their interrelated contexts work together to insure that success.

"In the traditional practices, the learner is responsible for his or her own learning, both in terms of content and method ... In the modern non-traditional practices ... the responsibility seems to have shifted from the learner to the teacher. The teacher takes on many of the decision-making responsibilities of the traditional learner as to what and how repertoire, technique and performance practices are to be learned."

Garrison says of Buddy's learning practice, "Buddy's natural talent, his fascination with the sound of the violin and his strong desire to learn to play were supported by a rich family neighborhood interest and involvement in the music. This combination of factors worked together to allow Buddy to achieve the status he has today in the eyes of his fellow fiddlers, that is the status of a 'master' Cape Breton fiddler."

His regular appearances in his native Cape Breton and his wonderful skill at performance have made him an idol for many musicians. Buddy is aware that he has had an influence upon many wonderful fiddlers who hold the tradition in their grasp today. Let's focus on Ashley MacIsaac, for example. MacIsaac demonstrates his insatiable musicianship on countless occasions. Early in his musical career, he acquired the capacity to absorb some of the finer points of the music tradition. His recording *fine thank you very much* (a traditional album) was released in 1996. Through this recording, he illustrates that he is very capable of playing the traditional music as others play it. As he renders "The Rosebud of Allenvale," "The Miller of Drone" and other selections including "Maggie Cameron" and "Barry's Trip to Paris" – all on one track – you can hear the influence Buddy has on Ashley's music. On the same recording, you can hear how Ashley interprets the performance style of other traditional players as well. (With tongue in cheek, he may be responding to his critics and their concern about how he interprets the old style, the old tunes.) Through his music, he illustrates that the traditional players represent many individual styles. Ashley has developed his unique style in technique, repertoire and performance.

Buddy has struck a chord among young and old musicians who eventually create their own distinctive sound and do so with the blessing of their idol. In Ashley's case, it is common knowledge that MacMaster has had a tremendous impact on shaping Ashley's music. One only has to note MacIsaac's repertoire, timing, drive, lift, bowing and, indeed, the passion in his music. But this emerges from Ashley's opportunity to study through observation Buddy's performances over several years while growing up in the nearby community of Creignish, a stone's throw from Judique.

In recent years, Buddy has had to succumb to the pressure to teach and has spent time at workshops demonstrating the art of teaching his style in fiddling. Preparing for a video with SeaBright Productions of Antigonish, producer Peter Murphy had the opportunity to be with Buddy when he was instructing a series of workshops at Sabhal Mòr Ostaig in Skye.

"I witnessed the immense respect and appreciation international audiences have for the soft-spoken man and his vibrant music," says Peter. "I have seen him teach a young Highlander in the Outer Hebrides, a classical violinist from England, a seasoned California musician, and his own fellow Cape Bretoners. He is equally at home no matter where or with whom he finds himself. He has no professional textbook or carefully rehearsed theatrical teaching style. His approach is natural and straightforward, and his vast knowledge of tunes and precise playing is what students seek – and treasure."

Buddy finds his own way to render his music. He learned through observation and participation, through trial and error. He has reflected on what it may have been like had he received instruction. One gets the impression from speaking with him that he would have enjoyed that opportunity but "I wasn't in the right place at the right time ... around here there was no one who could teach."

He is quick to suggest that the young fiddlers would be well-served if they took the time to work with someone who was trained in the classical sense but also had the capacity to render the music with the Gaelic flavour. For Buddy, living in an environment of the aural tradition provided him with the opportunity to master the instrument in the traditional way.

In the mid-1980s, Buddy began making appearances in the U.S. at some summer music camps and workshops for teaching fiddle. The camps, well-established when he was invited to participate, were attracting as many as two hundred or more learners at a variety of levels or performance competencies. By this time, fiddle music enthusiasts in the United States had become interested in the music of the Cape Breton fiddler, and fiddlers from a variety of genres now wanted to learn to play. Buddy was to become an icon at these camps or workshops and the American-style festivals.

In 1984, Buddy attended his first camp as an instructor at the Port Townsend Festival of American Fiddle Tunes in Washington State. He made the following comments in an interview with John Cable at CBC Sydney, one month prior to leaving for Washington. He had just returned from North Carolina, where he attended a popular three-day folk music festival.

"Well, we have been asked to go down there to instruct them ... show them the way we play the violin or fiddle in Cape Breton ... [The] Cape Breton style seems to be unique ... I understand it is quite popular on the west coast of the U.S.A. and maybe Canada ... In Scotland they play well ... They [are] more trained ... [They play] a lot of the style of J.S. Skinner ... [I am] looking forward to meeting with the different players and possibly picking up some pointers on their different styles of playing."

In 1985, he participated in the California Traditional Music Society Summer Solstice Festival in Los Angeles. In 1986, he made his first appearance at the Valley of the Moon Fiddle Camp (VOM), run by the popular Scottish fiddler Alasdair Fraser, and Buddy became a regular there for the next ten years.

The camp programs had several aspects in common. Some sessions placed a greater importance on teaching and repertoire, for example. In the teaching classes, the emphasis was on demonstration; in the repertoire session, the instructors performed a range of tunes as a full class. These could last up to ninety minutes. Additional classes were more like band labs. Students would organize in groups of their choice and any number of instruments and musical genres could be included in the sessions. The group would perform, to the extent that it was possible for learners, in unison playing select pieces. Other sessions would consist of a concert or recital or a dance setting where the guest artists would take centre stage and perform to a mixed audience. The camps ran full days until early evening and lasted generally for a week.

The Port Townsend workshop in Washington State is located at Fort Worden State Park. Located on an old American air force base, the setting had been used in the 1982 Richard Gere movie *An Officer and A Gentleman*. The multi-storey buildings were scattered throughout the old base and were huge in size. Classroom space was abundant. The setting was daunting for Buddy initially.

When Buddy arrived at this camp in 1984, it was his first venture at formal instruction. He understood the style of learning in the Cape Breton tradition and he also understood that the camp participants would be from different worlds in the musical sense. The challenge was immense as there were fiddlers, learning and teaching, from many fiddling styles found in the U.S. – Folk, Appalachian, Scottish, Irish, Cajun and Canadian. Buddy was invited to instruct in the Cape Breton style, of course. The understanding was that the teachers were not music teachers but rather tradition bearers. Learners were expected to apply whatever techniques they could to grasp the music, instruction and demonstrations being provided by the different instructors.

Marianne Jewell, a musician born in the U.S., has lived in Inverness, Cape Breton, since the early 1980s. She attended several camps where Buddy had been over the years. By 1981, she had already learned about his music from a well-informed Cape Breton network living on the west coast.

"I first met Buddy at St Ann's in 1983 ... I was hanging around with Father John Angus's [Rankin] family. They kind of adopted me the first years I came and they introduced me to Buddy. ... Even by this time, he was a hero in my eyes because I had a friend, Johnny Archie's [Mac-

Donald] son who was living on the west coast, and he was going to the workshops at Port Townsend and that's where I had gotten to know him [Johnny Archie's son] in 1981 and 1983 ... and he told me about Buddy and he played me some of his father's old tapes from early dances that Buddy was playing at [in Detroit] ... And he was his hero also and the more I heard about him the more I heard his playing ... the more ... this was the person that I wanted to hear ... and this was the goal! ... I met him at St Ann's as this was the first time that the Cape Breton Fiddlers' Association had their Scottish concert there."

Marianne explains that at the 1984 Port Townsend camp, organizers understood that the teaching routine would be a new experience for Buddy and so they planned to have musician Dave MacIsaac from Halifax attend to give Buddy some assistance. Dave had an excellent grasp of Buddy's style and the Cape Breton tradition generally. A well-known fiddler and guitarist who can play well in any number of styles, he is a rock, jazz and bluegrass performer as well. He has attended camps and festivals over the years and had a good insight as to what to expect at Port Townsend. The team approach worked well.

Dave MacIsaac explains in an interview on the same CBC program that featured Buddy: "Certain classes are called repertoire sessions. Buddy will start and play what he wants ... name some tunes and where they come from. Students will have tape recorders and will take notes in the classroom situation ... [In] other classes, they will share extra tunes and explain bowing and fingering techniques."

MacIsaac would speak to a feature or particular aspect of the music. He would then ask Buddy to demonstrate that piece or phrase. The technique was, essentially, to have the students learn a phrase within a particular tune, one phrase at a time, and to build upon that process. There would be no written material initially. As the students learned a sense of the melody by ear, then they would get a written sheet so that they could further practise the music. The emphasis, however, was to encourage the students to watch bowing and positioning and to listen carefully for the embellishments and ornamentation. From time to time, Buddy would briefly comment on the tune titles and perhaps the composer.

Culture clash was guaranteed to be part of these workshops. In some instances, Buddy was asked to play for contra dancers, for example, during the week-long activities. In that particular dance tradition, it is imperative that the music performed consists of thirty-two bars. This was not a problem for Buddy, of course. Initially, Buddy had introduced tunes that had only sixteen bars, and he would then simply add another sixteen bars, thus playing a second melody. But the transition to another melody was confusing for the contra dancers even though it was common in the Cape Breton dance tradition. In time, Buddy made the adjustment and recognized the need to play tunes that fit the manner the contra dance prescribed.

Also, in the Cape Breton tradition, the step dancers are expected to complete their routine and then stop dancing and, at that point, the fiddler then stops. In the American camp setting, it was not unusual for Buddy to encounter step dancers who would simply keep going until the fiddler would stop. That is not what Buddy was accustomed to, so he would play and play and seemingly never tire. In time, the dancers began to realize Buddy was not going to stop, so they had to stop first and then move on. Next dancer, please!

The clash was a bit subtler when it came to the more technical aspects of certain tunes. Marianne Jewell explains the kind of situation Buddy faced at some camps, especially where the learners were more adept musicians in their musical genre. When the students were invited to observe Buddy playing the reels "Red Shoes" and "Tom Rae," they were faced with another illustration of culture clash. Pianist Barbara MacDonald-Magone and fiddler Carl MacKenzie accompanied Buddy at this particular camp in 1985.

Marianne Jewell says, "There is a note in the pipe scale ... not the usual one that you hear flatted but the third note of the pipe scale ... It's not quite a C-sharp and it's not a C-natural – it's like in-between ... And a lot of fiddlers [who] were influenced by the pipes played that note or learned it from a fiddler that did ... This is the way that both Carl and Buddy were doing it. They were playing that note ... you might call it in the cracks ... because a piano doesn't have those microtones ... So the discussion came up among the participants, 'Are you playing a C-sharp or a C-natural?' ... and Buddy looks at Carl and Carl looks at Buddy and they start playing it again. 'Well, this is what we are playing' ... Both of them just played it again ... expecting that you would know again ... This went on for about twenty minutes ... Barb was getting a little bit exasperated and she said, 'This is the way they do it in Cape Breton – right ... saying I'll choose a C-sharp or I'll chose a C-natural, you know, it doesn't really matter."

In 1986, Buddy was invited for the first time to the Valley of the Moon (VOM) music camp. Initially started as a rather rustic camp, with a very informal setting, it evolved as a serious place for learning. Marianne Jewell explains, "It did not have the 1960s feel, as was the case with [American] Fiddle Tunes camp [at Port Townsend]." The VOM was designed to teach Scottish fiddle music in particular and as such the program featured instructors from Scotland as well as Buddy and Alasdair Fraser. The classes were set up according to the speed or ease at which the individual fiddlers would learn a tune – from slow to supersonic. Buddy's experience at Fiddle Tunes camp had begun to serve him well by this time. He had developed a high level of patience and a way to highlight the progress being made, no matter how poorly a student may be doing at the camp.

A student experience is nicely described by Mark Luther, who attended a VOM camp. Mark recalls, "I first met Buddy MacMaster at Valley of the Moon in 1997. Although I was a beginner, not really qualified to sit in his classes, I couldn't resist, knowing his reputation and not knowing if I'd ever have the opportunity again. I eagerly sat in the front row, and Buddy was so conscientious that he would repeat passages over and over, noticing that I wasn't getting it. I finally had to say to him, 'Buddy, I'm here in awe to watch you play and teach, but I can't keep up, please don't force the whole class to learn at my level.' He of course smiled in his warm way.

"It was my and my kids' experiences at Valley of the Moon that directly inspired us to start Rocky Mountain Fiddle Camp [RMFC in Colorado] in 1999.

"We were modeled after VOM, so I hoped to invite some of the great teachers who had taught there. I asked Buddy two or three times, but it wasn't until 2001 that he was able to come. Due to the work involved in running the camp, I had not and to this day have not sat through a single complete class, with the one exception of one of Buddy's classes, and I proudly announced to him and the class that in years (at that time three, now going on nine) of managing fiddle camp, it was my first and only time.

"That was his only time at RMFC. We would be very happy to have Buddy back again at RMFC."

Mary Janet MacDonald is an icon in the Cape Breton step-dance tradition. She attended several Valley of the Moon camps as a dance instructor. Her first was in 1989. Buddy would have attended several camps by that time. Mary Janet has known Buddy all her adult life and he is always her fiddler of choice for dancing. She was amazed by the respect that all the participants had for Buddy.

"Not that I was surprised in any way, shape or form at the respect that these people had [for him]. But [when] you see it first-hand ... I think so often when you take something right at home for granted and people like him for granted. It was so interesting for me to see the awe that people had for him that far away from home – that they knew him in California – to see the admiration and respect they had for him ... it had been going on all along ... just to see him so laidback in his classes.

"He had a special rapport with the young students. Laura Risk is one name I can recall. Now these students are well-known fiddlers with various Celtic groups and have made a name for themselves. Buddy was so good and relaxed with them. They just loved him. He made time for them. It was so nice to see that and to see the respect that they had for him. He still gets a kick that people treat him with such respect and that he is so well-known and he is over eighty."

In a CBC interview, Buddy comments on his enthusiasm for the youth learning the music: "I think it is just great that there is so much interest now ... fiddling and step-dancing and singing has come a long way the last few years ... the interest ... and so many young people playing now ... and most of them are very talented ... and they start young."

Barbara MacDonald-Magone, who attended VOM camps as a piano

accompanist during Buddy's earlier visits, describes his approach to the class sessions this way. "He taught [fiddle] by example in that he would play a phrase or tune over and over until the students got it. [The students] found out quickly that if they asked questions, the information was forthcoming ... Rather than talk about it, he would go on to play it again and again until they could hear or see the particular embellishment or fingering or bow stroke ... Buddy has always been a champion of musicians just starting out, quietly encouraging them and teaching them by example."

The students would sit in a semicircle at Buddy's feet and place their tape recorders in a variety of positions to capture Buddy's music and use the tape collected to help them learn the tunes following the sessions. Subsequently, video recording began to edge into the circle. Students were determined to position cameras directly in Buddy's face. Initially, Buddy was accepting of the practice until he was asked specifically whether this was any bother. He was as forthcoming on that issue as he was to questions about the music. "*Oh, yes!*" was his immediate reply. When it was pointed out to the students that the practice of recording during classes was inhibiting for Buddy, as it would be for any musician, steps were taken to curtail the habit.

If video was inhibiting for Buddy in the class sessions, his inhibitions were less so when it came time to join in the early evening fun among the instructors and camp workers. The participants described him as a "great sport!"

Barbara MacDonald-Magone explains, "We were able to convince him to dress up as a compatriot of [Scottish composer] Niel Gow complete with white tights, knee-length velvet pants, a ruffled shirt and a period jacket. He really enjoyed it ... Alasdair [Fraser] was Niel Gow that year.

"[On another occasion] Brendan [Barbara's son] was able to convince Buddy to don loud, blue plaid, flannel overalls with one strap hanging down, L.A. style, a black, snug t-shirt, high-top white sneakers, beads around his neck, a baseball cap backwards, sunglasses and a boom box on his shoulder. Buddy entered the room weaving and bobbing to hip-hop music and doing a modern dance routine along with a bit of lip-sync without knowing any of the words ... When it became understood who this rap singer character was ... the room exploded with laughter and cameras flashing. He was so good-natured about all of these shenanigans and seemed so pleased to be a part of them. He has a devilish side. He's never unkind – just funny."

Mary Janet recalls her own experience with this other side of Buddy at the special fun sessions, which had been well-embedded by the time she had made her way to VOM. This particular occasion was a fundraiser for scholarships for young students by way of a silent auction. The star of this particular auction was going to be Buddy MacMaster – out of character! So Buddy was expected to do something he had not done before.

"My job that year, with help from my friend Mary Lamey, was to get Buddy ready in costume because he was going to be the ultimate auction prize. This was the outfit: we had pantyhose which he put on ... not a problem ... he had big blue, high-heel shoes and they were a bright blue ... the skirt that he had on came down to mid-calf and it was red with black rippling through it. He had slipped into an adjoining room to put on some of this stuff, of course, and returned with a top that was a black lacey teddy with a full cup ... However, there is nothing in the cup until we blew up these pink balloons. 'Put them in the right way, now,' he said, laughing aloud.

"Mary and I were so sore from laughing. He was getting into the part and it was so friggin' funny ... Then we put this wig on him ... brown long locks of curls ... Then I did the make-up. I emphasized the eye shadow and some nice black eyebrows, red, red, cheeks and the reddest lipstick I could find ... He had a red purse ... Then he walked around just like a woman in the little cottage we were in ... it was within walking distance of the big hall ... and now he had to wait for his cue to enter. We scattered and went in and sat down ... In walks Buddy MacMaster 'The final entertainer for the evening' ... They had no clue that this was Buddy MacMaster ... He waltzed in and greeted and nodded at everybody ... the wrists were really flinging ... and away he went ... up the front and back.

"Then the ripple happened. They now realized that it was Buddy. They were screaming and the cameras were flashing ... Buddy even opened up the purse and threw out some of its contents. At that point I lost it ... I don't know how much money they made that evening but they did well on auctioning off the costume that Buddy had been wearing ...

Buddy was just someone who never ceased to amaze them.

"He was at home there as if he did it everyday. A lot of people don't know the humorous side of Buddy. To see him especially with his family [at home] ... his sisters ... they are all such good laughers ... at the greatest things ... they have such fun and life."

Mary Janet remembers a special jaunt with Buddy. She discusses a trip to Utah, outside Salt Lake City, to Sundance, which has an association with American actor Robert Redford. It had been developed to provide a training base for young budding actors. The family of Alex Bigney, the well-known American artist, came to know Buddy. They had a particular interest in folk music. The family also has a link with the now extinct place Kirkmint, once an active community near New Glasgow, Nova Scotia. They had a fondness for the fiddle and other acoustic instruments and had taken Buddy to their home on many occasions to give private lessons to the children. The children are active performers today and have recorded several CDs.

Mary Janet shares the following: "Robert Redford had become so interested in these kids' music and he would bring them to entertain at different functions that he would have. So he wanted to do whatever he could to see that this music that they loved to do could be done by other people. So he offered up this Sundance facility to the Bigneys to invite others to learn fiddle. So they brought Alasdair [Fraser], Barbara [MacDonald-Magone], Buddy and I to teach. It was on a much smaller scale than VOM. But again the great respect for Buddy. All the people who came there knew all about Buddy. It was amazing. They hung on to every word that came out of Buddy's mouth. And I don't even think that he realized that, you know. They just wanted to talk to him ... be up close and personal. Just great respect again. So that was really nice to be a part of that and to be able to just see him and to stand back and watch him in action. In all of that he was just being himself. It was just beautiful to see.

"To travel with him is a joy. He just knows what he was doing. He is a well-travelled soul. He is a great companion. He would always be talking about who you are and your people. And he was so clannish about all the people that mean a lot to him – his parents and his grandparents. He took you under his wing. He is so kind."

Barbara shares a similar view: "Many times at other venues when we met, Buddy and I would talk quietly about Cape Breton and the news, and perhaps the bygone days. It was exquisite sharing these talks with Buddy, for I gained a whole new insight into who he is. He always explained the genealogy to me if I were talking about people from Cape Breton. In fact, he would pre-empt his story to interrupt it to make sure I understood [the genealogy]. I appreciate this, for I have a lifelong interest in who belongs to whom."

As if to come full circle in the exchange with Mary Janet MacDonald, she describes a concert at Kintyre Farm in Inverness County, Cape Breton, in August 2006. Buddy was one of the performers.

"It was held inside the hall because of the chance of rain. I had the pleasure of introducing Buddy ... He was at the side door that leads to the stage ... From Buddy's vantage point, he could see only part of the audience. But what can you say to introduce Buddy MacMaster? ... There is so much to say ... so, I thought I would ask if there was anyone in the audience who did not know Buddy ... Then I would speak to them ... so I asked and there were about six from the full audience who had not ... so I said '...this is for you' ... I gave a little snapshot about Buddy ... But from my husband's [Cecil] vantage point backstage, he could see only the one hand in the air. With that, he turned to Buddy who was standing next to him and said, 'Buddy, look at that. There is one person out there who does not know you.' Buddy replies, 'There's only one. Is there?' ... in his slow distinctive brogue but in his greatest humble tone, of course.

"And you rarely hear him with an off day. He played at that concert with the same grace that he did twenty years ago ... Once he gets going, he's just like the Eveready Battery ... He finished the first set and then he announced that he would like to play another one ... and he came out with a set of jigs ... and there were a couple of jigs that I never heard before ... He's still learning new tunes ... It is amazing . . ."

In an interview, Jody Stecher explains Buddy's popularity as a performer at the camp concerts in particular. "Buddy always got the most encores at a concert with other fiddlers. We are talking about really good fiddlers. Like the prize-winning fiddlers from Scotland – from the East and the North. He always worked hard at getting his music just right. He really worked on specific sets. He would really make it special. So, he got the most encores, partly because it was Buddy that was the hero but also because he was competitive enough to make sure that his music merited those encores."

Marianne Jewell observes that people who met Buddy at different venues, wherever they were located, were absolutely in awe of him and the words most often used to describe him are "dearly loved." Allan MacLeod of Inverness, Scotland, expresses the same sentiments: "Wherever he has played – whether in Inverness, Uist, Harris or as a guest of Celtic Connections on a big stage in Glasgow – the reception which Buddy has received from his audience has always been enthusiastic and appreciative. His playing contains so much happiness, reflecting his kind heart, and that cheerful message always gets across."

Buddy has made numerous trips to Scotland. His first visit was in 1970, but he and his music were well-known among many in Scotland before then. It was then that he met Scottish fiddler Hector McAndrew, who had already made an impression among Cape Breton fiddlers.

Buddy recalls, "Hector and his wife were about to leave the house when we arrived. It was like at home as we came unannounced. We were travelling with Ron Gonella [the Scottish fiddler]. Father John Angus Rankin and Marie [Buddy's wife] were with me. Anyway, they invited us in and we settled down for a lovely afternoon of music. She made some tea and lunch. I recall Hector played for a long time that afternoon. He was very knowledgeable of the music and had a great deal of interest in the Cape Breton style, too. His own music is close to the Cape Breton style – lots of depth. It was a sweet music, yet he had a nice drive and life to his music. You could hear the Gaelic influence. And he enjoyed the tunes from the books, too. He was so smooth and so natural. I think he was one of the great players from the Old Country. But I thoroughly enjoyed the session. It was one of my most enjoyable occasions with the music."

BBC Radio producer Norman MacDonald recalls, "I first became aware of Buddy MacMaster as a significant contributor to the Gaelic diaspora when I joined the staff of the BBC in Glasgow on my leaving university in 1974. The head of things at that time was the late Fred MacAulay, who had visited Cape Breton not long before, and Buddy and Winnie Chafe were among those people whom he had recorded; their style of music, to say nothing of their names, was completely new to all of us at the time. We played them a lot on our programmes and were amazed at the interest which they engendered. I remember a knowledge-able musician saying to me at the time that their music had 'a rawness and a sweetness at the same time and Scotland has nothing like it in terms of its sprightliness.' That seemed like the ultimate compliment.

"On moving to live in Cape Breton in 1978, I soon got used to know-ing of Buddy's standing. In a milieu where violin music dominated every-thing it was odd to think that we could attend dances at Glencoe Mills on a summer's evening and listen to Buddy play. We tried to persuade our many visitors from Scotland that a stay-over for a Thursday night was imperative and never was it more truly said than that; that element of Cape Breton in the '70s and '80s was more Scottish than Scotland!

"Buddy's status at the heart of Cape Breton music was confirmed with a glittering testimonial in the old Adult Vocational Training Centre building [now the Nova Scotia Community College, Marconi Campus] at which I had the honour to act as M.C. These were heady days with Cape Breton's musicians established as national names both in Scotland and in Canada. The many visiting TV crews from Scotland all had a ses-sion with Buddy at the top of their lists."

In 1975, Buddy visited Scotland for the second time. On this occa-sion, he was in the company of several musicians from both sides of the water. The Honorable Allan J. MacEachen, then Secretary of State for the Government of Canada, invited musicians from Nova Scotia to perform at Edinburgh Castle. Scottish officials hosted the function and it was the first official ceilidh ever held at the castle.

When Buddy returned to Scotland in 1979, it was a trip that had been organized by Norman MacDonald. Norman recalls, "Of course, I had the great privilege in 1979 of being part of bringing Buddy MacMas-ter and Scotland together again. He became part of the tour, which I helped organise, which brought the Sons of Skye and a galaxy of other Cape Breton stars, not just to Glasgow, Edinburgh and Inverness but to the National Mod in Stornoway. Looking back on it, it is interesting to assess what an important role that trip played in the development of the current relations between Cape Breton and the Highlands of Scotland. The way Buddy and his compatriots were received on Scotland's stages confirmed that a new relationship between the Old and the New Countries was underway.

"I remember one late evening in Stornoway a local worthy, slightly the worse for wear, hovering around our minibus and being attracted by the signage and exclaiming, 'Sons of Skye, aye, Skye, I've been there; Kyleakin, a great place for pubs!' The old Skye and Cape Breton have been less easily confused as a result of the furrows ploughed in those days."

On this tour, Buddy was accompanied by fiddler Carl MacKenzie, pianist Doug MacPhee, Gaelic singer Father Allan MacMillan (the current parish priest at St Andrew's Church, Judique) and well-known Gaelic storyteller Joe Neil MacNeil. The musicians made a recording with BBC Radio, produced by Allan MacDonald, at the Drumossie Motel in Inverness. At other venues, Scottish fiddlers Tom Anderson and Ally Bain of the Shetlands performed with Buddy and Carl MacKenzie. Buddy and Carl visited the gravesite of famous fiddler/composer James Scott Skinner before returning to Cape Breton.

While in Inverness, Scotland, in 1991, Buddy visited the home of Scottish fiddler Allan MacLeod and began a treasured friendship that remains today. The demand to have Buddy teach the Cape Breton style fiddling to musicians in Scotland would soon begin to take root.

Allan says, "Buddy first visited our home in Inverness, Scotland, October 1991. He was on a Scottish tour of Highland venues with the California-based Scottish fiddler Alasdair Fraser and pianist Barbara Magone ... Buddy stayed at our house and, of course, we had a wonderful party in the Cape Breton style after his concert in Inverness ... Later, when I heard home recordings of Buddy playing at house parties in Cape Breton and the States in the 1950s onwards I realized that we had had one of those magical evenings in our home."

Buddy began to teach at the Sabhal Mòr Ostaig, the Gaelic College in Skye, in July 1992. Alasdair Fraser had established the program in

1986, following his successful Valley of the Moon camps in California. Allan MacLeod explained that Donnie Campbell, a Gaelic speaker who had a special interest in the shared culture between Scotland and Cape Breton, was instrumental in organizing the short courses. The Skye program attracted considerable interest in Scotland especially and from a range of music genres. Fraser had encouraged a greater emphasis on an old style of fiddling, one that he had acquired from his visits to Cape Breton over the years. (Fraser gave a highly acclaimed performance at the twenty-fifth annual Big Pond Summer Festival in Cape Breton in 1989.)

MacLeod notes that "by the time Buddy came over in 1992 the course in Skye was attracting some of the best Scottish traditional players as well as a crop of enthusiastic youngsters, all of whom appreciated not only Buddy's manner of playing his Cape Breton style but also its direct derivation from Scottish playing for dance." MacLeod adds, "The music courses were complemented each day by step dance tutoring from Harvey Beaton, Port Hastings, Cape Breton, so that the fiddlers came to appreciate the requirements of step-dancing."

MacLeod continues: "Buddy was instantly loved by the audience and students for his quiet but authorative manner in the style of a Highland gentleman and of course his wonderful music.

"From these fiddle and step dance courses in Skye which were taught by Buddy and Harvey until 2002, there emerged a new generation of youngsters who are now leading the way in Scottish traditional music and dance. Buddy and Harvey inspired not only the active teaching generation who cascaded the Cape Breton style throughout Scotland but also the teenagers and younger [children] who are now amongst the best performers in the country. There are very few traditional players or step dancers in today's Scotland who have not been influenced by Cape Bretoners – particularly Buddy and Harvey.

"The courses at Skye also influenced the establishment of other courses such as the Ceolas Course on South Uist and the Taransay Fiddle Camp near Harris. Buddy has taught at both of these as well as giving day workshops at the end of his teaching week in places such as Inverness."

In the course of Buddy's visits, Sabhal Mòr Ostaig has grown from its original stone barn to an extended building with residential accommodation and additional teaching and performance buildings, with probably more to follow as it establishes itself at university standard in the study and teaching of Scottish Gaelic and culture.

Allan shares a rather humorous incident about Buddy and his teaching at Skye. "While the building work was going on sometimes his class would take their chairs and move outside to take advantage of the warm sunshine (yes, these days do occur in Scotland!). On one of those days there was a joiner [carpenter] working with a hammer on the wooden roof trusses. He was totally oblivious to his surroundings and took no notice of the fiddlers but after a short time Buddy noticed that he was hammering with a very regular beat so before we knew it we were playing the march in time with the joiner! It was very funny and a good example of Buddy's gentle sense of humour."

Allan speaks highly of his association with Buddy. "One of my fondest memories of Buddy's trips to Skye was the year we organized a West Mabou style family square dance in the Ardvasar village hall near the Gaelic College. We agreed that only Inverness County Square Sets should be danced throughout the evening and that we should be strict about keeping it to four couples per set. Buddy played for most of the sets while Jackie Dunn played piano, with the Scottish [fiddle] player Karen Steven – who had learned from Buddy – giving him a spell. Rae MacColl from Skye, who had learned to stepdance in Cape Breton, called the dances.

"We had set a modest admission charge but the turnout was so good that we had a packed dance floor all evening, dancing six sets, and made enough money on the gate to give the players some reward. Everybody had a wonderful time and we even had some individual dancers showing their steps at a halfway interval. As far as I am aware this has been the only occasion when a strictly Cape Breton style square dance has been held in Scotland." (Author's note: the Gaelic Society of Cape Breton organized a visit to Scotland in October 1973. The society's membership presented Cape Breton ceilidhs with milling frolics and square dances featuring fiddlers, singers and dancers who were visiting the Islands to reconnect with long-lost cousins. The Gaelic Society's square dance routine focused on the Cape Breton County style, however.)

MacLeod describes Buddy's affection for the people with whom he met and spent time chatting. "Away from the fiddle, I have seen him take an interest in talking to non-musicians in the local areas, such as a fellow by the surname Currie in South Uist whose relatives had immigrated to Cape Breton. Similarly with people of [the] MacMaster surname from the Moidart area. He was always very interested in talking to my mother when she was alive, seeing the similarity no doubt in her Hebridean manner to womenfolk in Cape Breton of the last generation."

In the company of young or old alike, Buddy can wow any audience. Liz Doherty is a well-known Irish fiddler from Donegal, who has visited Cape Breton on numerous occasions to perform and to research some of the finer points of the Cape Breton music tradition. She has a doctoral degree in music from University of Limerick, Ireland.

Liz recalls a memorable experience about Buddy: "One of the most extraordinary musical events I ever experienced was a concert held in Glasgow in 2001 as part of the Celtic Connections festival program. Beolach – Wendy MacIsaac, Mairi Rankin, Mac Morin, Matthew Foulds, Patrick Gillis and Ryan MacNeil – had recently formed and was sharing the bill for an afternoon concert in the Strathclyde Suite with Buddy MacMaster and a host of accompanists – Joey Beaton, Betty Lou Beaton and Dave MacIsaac – in celebration of Buddy's album release, *The Judique Flyer*. Beolach took to the stage first and gave an amazing performance. From the very first note, the atmosphere was electric; the crowd loved them; the place was rocking. I remember thinking, 'Poor Buddy. He'll never be able to follow this.' How wrong I was!

"Out came the master himself, looking dapper as ever in his suit, taking his time getting settled, acknowledging the audience with a shy smile and nod of the head. He lifted the fiddle, tucked it under his chin, and began what was one of the most captivating afternoons of fiddle music, ever. From soaring airs to pounding strathspeys that tipped over into the liveliest of reels, Buddy performed set after set from an extensive repertoire. In between, he would talk a little bit about the tunes – where they came from, who collected them, what book he found them in – displaying a seriously impressive knowledge of the tradition. And he talked about Cape Breton, and life on the island, and the strength of the connections with Scotland through the music and the dance and the language. And he drew the people in, deeper and deeper. They were spellbound. Mesmerized. Enchanted.

"With Buddy and with his music – and indeed the two are as one – the full range of emotions is there: the dignity; the humour; the passion; the sense of pride he displays, in that typically understated way, in being a bearer of the tradition. The great Scottish fiddler, Hector MacAndrew, once told Winston Fitzgerald that his [Winston's] playing was 'very close to the truth.' On that January afternoon in Glasgow, Buddy MacMaster's performance was, most definitely, the truth. It was a privilege to experience it."

Norman MacDonald recalls his meeting with Buddy while Buddy was in Scotland to provide instructional classes in 2002; he was reflecting on meeting Buddy some twenty-three years earlier.

Norman says, "It is odd to think that I stood again on the glorious, though now uninhabited, Hebridean island of Taransay in the summer of 2002. Standing with me was Buddy MacMaster and I had come to interview him about the summer school which he was conducting on the island. His presence gave this most unique of all summer school settings an awesome feeling. The few minutes of our recorded conversation are among the most memorable which I have broadcast in my long years in the business.

"Buddy's unique brand of modesty and his own dedication to passing on the music and to seeing young people enjoying it will always stay with me. He is one of the Gaelic diaspora's real celebrities in the nicest possible way, and a man of genius ahead of his time."

Janine Randall was born in Boston but has deep Inverness County roots. Her father, Johnny Muise, who had left Cape Breton to work in Boston after the Second World War, was a good friend of Buddy's. Johnny quickly became immersed in the Cape Breton music scene that had been developed in Boston by that time. He maintained that interest throughout his life and he instilled in his family an interest in the music and the Inverness County connection. Sessions of music in the home were common and summer trips to Inverness were routine.

Janine explains, "I knew many of the great fiddlers who were living in Boston, like Angus Chisholm and Bill Lamey. They were good friends

Internationally acclaimed violinist Natalie MacMaster, visiting with her Uncle Buddy.

Dave MacIsaac with Buddy at the Port Townsend American Fiddle Tunes Camp, 1984.

Buddy with Alasdair Fraser, a renowned Scottish fiddler, at Sabhal Mòr Ostaig in Skye, Scotland, 1992.

Buddy playing tunes for step dancer Harvey Beaton of Port Hastings at Sabhal Mòr Ostaig in Skye, Scotland 1992.

of my dad especially. And my mom played piano for many of the fiddlers. And Mary Jessie MacDonald, a great piano player, would also visit. So by the time I was a young adult, I had already acquired an interest in the music and learned to play piano, too. I came to know the music of fiddlers like Jerry Holland as well. And Buddy was always part of that network. He would visit Boston to perform at dances and concerts.

"But I really got to know Buddy well in later years when I opened up the Ceilidh Trail School of Celtic Music in Inverness. My husband, Ken, and I purchased an old schoolhouse in Inverness in the mid-'90s and invested in making it a place where the music could be taught. One of the first people I wanted involved in the school was Buddy. He agreed to attend and teach his style of fiddling. He had developed a good reputation from having visited music camps in the U.S. and Scotland by that time. So, Buddy was an important person in helping draw people to Cape Breton to learn the music. And he understood the importance of having people visit Cape Breton and to spend time on the island and how that would help contribute to the local economy. He understood that very well.

"He spent a wonderful ten years at the Ceilidh School. He never missed a session. He was a great teacher. He recognized that this would be part of his legacy. He had students from Japan, Australia, Scotland, the U.S. and Canada, and they would be playing tunes that he had taught them at the Ceilidh School. That makes me feel proud, too.

"One evening we were in a side classroom while a recital program was underway at the school. In the room with me were Dwayne Cote, Richard Wood and Brenda Stubbert – all great fiddlers who were involved in teaching sessions at the school. We were quietly chatting when suddenly we heard a certain piece of music being played. None of us had heard the tune before. I looked to the side and there was Buddy playing this music. We all looked at each other. We realized that this was just remarkable. Later I learned that Buddy had acquired the tune from a visit to Scotland the previous summer. So even at his age he was still learning new tunes and teaching new stuff. I think that is a marvelous thing to say about Buddy. He just pops out new stuff as well as the old. He is always learning. That's what makes him so young at heart."

Subsequent to establishing the school, Janine had the opportunity to accompany Buddy during some of his concert tours. A memorable occasion in 2001 took Buddy, Janine and several other musicians into Montana and later into the Yukon to perform. While in the Yukon, Buddy had a chance to talk to people about early mining there. His father, John Duncan, had worked in the Yukon years before. Janine came to realize that the visit had a special meaning for Buddy. She recalls, "I did not know about his father's connection with the mining work in that area. When we went there, he became a little teary-eyed and told us about his father having worked there many years ago. And that this was his first visit to the Yukon. We had not realized before actually arriving that this place was important in that way to Buddy."

Buddy recalls, "Well, it was nice to visit the Yukon. I know how hard my father had worked in that area, just as he did in Timmins. The mines were difficult to work in at that time ... and I suppose at any time. But he was so far away from home and things were tough. So when I went to the Yukon for the first time to play my music, it was something very special."

Janine then described a fundraising experience with Buddy. In the late 1990s, St. Francis Xavier University established a travel bursary program to support students' interest, province-wide, to visit the U.K. to further learn about Gaelic culture. To raise money for the program, the university officials struck a committee. Buddy was asked to join along with other celebrated personalities, including the Rev. Malcolm MacDonell, Sister Margaret MacDonell, Allan J. MacEachen, Ken Nilsen and John Buchanan. The committee continues to meet and is chaired by Rev. Vernon Boutilier, who actually initiated the program. Janine was asked if she might organize a dance in Boston to raise money; she agreed.

She explains, "I called Buddy to ask if he would play the dance as he was on the board. He said that he would be happy to help. I started passing the word around and we got a lot of support from other fiddlers. They knew people at the *Boston Globe* and the *Boston Herald*. The Canadian American Club donated the hall. And we put on this huge dance. And the money was raised for the Scottish Bursary program at St. F.X. I understand it was a nice kick-start to the money-raising effort. And it helped create an awareness of the program. Since its inception, many students have been able to visit Scotland and Ireland with the assistance of the bursary program."

Defining Tradition

Buddy MacMaster's music is rooted in tradition as it relates to both Scotland and Cape Breton. As a matter of fact, Buddy best defines that tradition. He is valued in the context of three important and distinct eras of the music in particular: first, the Golden Age of fiddling in Scotland from about 1730 to 1820; second, Cape Breton's First Golden Age from 1920 to 1969; and third, from 1970 to the present, which is commonly understood as an era of revivalism, Cape Breton's Second Golden Age. Buddy Mac-Master is vital to today's understanding of these eras as he is the most important link to each. As such, he is due recognition by the current generation of traditional musicians as well as the proponents for maintaining the tradition such as community activists and educators, who are well-served by acknowledging Buddy's longstanding approach to the music.

In the first timeline (1730-1820), the national music in Scotland itself had enjoyed a rebirth of interest. There were a series of initiatives to collect, publish and promote the music. Compositions by the great masters of the period, Niel Gow (1727-1807) and William Marshall (1748-1833), were published. (Later, works by James Scott Skinner [1843-1927] were published for distribution and they remain vital to Buddy's music also, perhaps more so than the earlier initiatives.)

Buddy's connection with this era is through the music of these early composers and is well-documented. His research into and acquisition of the music demonstrates this connection clearly. Buddy could also draw on other composers of that era.

Music scholar James Hunter writes, "The first publication of fiddle music per se was a collection of *Scots Reels or Country Dances* published in Edinburgh by Robert Bremner (1757). A profusion of collections followed from all over the country, most of them including original compositions in the traditional style..."

Also of importance in this era was the work by collectors like Captain Simon Fraser (1773-1852), for example, whose efforts resulted in an extensive compilation of the old Gaelic melodies. The preface to the 1874 edition of Fraser's work says, "An enthusiastic lover of music, the Captain early set himself to collect the sweet melodies of his native Highlands, – noting down the airs as sung around the hearth on winter nights, or on summer evenings." These older tunes of Scotland, which were once of the aural tradition and had become threatened and indeed abandoned by some, were published incorporating the tempered scales. Thus they were more prone to losing their Gaelic flavour despite the Captain's efforts and noble intentions. For these reasons, the music in Scotland changed, despite Gow's suggestion, as outlined by James Hunter, that standardization had not occurred: "In every part of Scotland where we have occasionally been, and from every observation we were able to make, [we] have not once met with two professional musicians who played the same notes of any tune." What were the non-professionals playing, one might ask?

Richard Blaustein's succinct account of the initial revivalism of the national music in Scotland also illustrates that a decline started by 1820, however. He explains that this was a result of less interest by the "High society, which had so ardently patronized and supported traditional music and dancing." But by the 1880s, a series of strathspey and reel societies emerged with the objective to keep the national music of Scotland alive. Among the early icons in this effort was a young Niel Gow, who won a fiddling contest that resulted in a patronage appointment by the Duke of Athol. This process remained active with the establishment of additional societies and contests until 1937. Beginning in 1969 through to

1977, major contests were reestablished in Scotland to foster interest in and support for the national music. Blaustein further comments, "These groups, which feature large numbers of fiddlers playing written arrangements of fiddle tunes under the direction of conductors, are still quite popular in Scotland [today]."

One result, however, of the efforts to stimulate an interest in the fiddle music in Scotland through collecting and composing for publication, patronizing, contests and societies was that the old Gaelic style music would change. Some would argue that it disappeared, at least in the fiddling tradition. Studies in Scotland, Ireland and the United States conclude, as explained in Blaustein's research, "We observe elaborate, standardized contest or exhibition styles seemingly submerging older, more localized repertoires and performance technique." In Scotland, the fiddle music especially would now evolve into a more restrictive and homogeneous style. Dr. Angus MacDonald, champion piper from Glenuig, Scotland, and former resident of Cape Breton, in his article, "In Defense of Scotland's Piping Tradition," is quick to remind the Gaels on both sides of the water that the piping tradition in Scotland has remained solid, firm and traditional with its own unique blend of Gaelic flavour.

Burt Feintuch writes in his liner notes for the 2003 recording *Buddy MacMaster – Cape Breton Tradition*, "Cape Bretoners claim that their music is an older form of Scottish tradition than what you hear these days in Scotland, and many Scots would seem to agree, as they started inviting Buddy MacMaster to spend summer weeks in places such as Uist and Skye, teaching Scots to play old Scottish music."

Through Buddy MacMaster, one can appreciate the significance of the Scottish development to the Cape Breton scene. This is especially true in the proliferation of the written music that had been collected and published for use in the societies and contests throughout Scotland. Eventually, these collections would make their way to Cape Breton, but in the absence of efforts to standardize the music performance.

While the Golden Age of Scottish Fiddling in Scotland was expanding and then waning, the music in Cape Breton was steeped still in the old tradition. Subsequently, by the 1920s Cape Breton had matured its own tradition. It nurtured the old repertoire and developed techniques that had been carefully crafted, thereby creating a distinctive sound. For Buddy MacMaster, the sound is imperative. "My positioning [holding bow and fiddle, and finger placement] is what I have seen among the older players in Inverness County and it always seems to let me go to where I want to go."

Buddy's approach to his music is one that has its genesis first among the Gaelic-speaking Scots who immigrated from the Highlands and the Western Isles to Cape Breton in the late eighteenth and early nineteenth centuries. These Gaels were not ambassadors of the early Scottish publications, contests and societies. In Cape Breton, transmitting the music from fiddler to fiddler from community to community through the aural tradition – including songs and *Puirt A Beul* (mouth music/jigging) and through the style of playing maintained within the bagpiping tradition – had remained the primary means of sharing and preserving the music. As a result, an old style of playing remained an integral feature of the Cape Breton fiddling – spontaneous, lively and with access to lots of old tunes with a great lift for dancing. This is Buddy's music.

Buddy has his own view on the differences in the music style: "I hate to see the music evolve into something that does not resemble what our ancestors brought here. Fiddling in Cape Breton is unique. Perhaps the fact that people weren't coming here to work and stuff kept the unique style. Other areas lost some of the Scottish style because of so many people moving in. There is a big Irish influence now and a little French. They have great music and I love it and there is room for both, but I would hate for fiddlers to lose the old Scottish style that was unique to Inverness County and Cape Breton."

By the 1940s, the first published collection of Cape Breton compositions, *Cape Breton Scottish Melodies* edited by Gordon F. MacQuarrie, became available. Reading music was still rare among fiddlers but many would persevere to learn and, indeed, adapt. In doing so, they would be able to access the tunes that were to become available not only through local composers like Gordon MacQuarrie and Sandy MacLean, among many others, but also from the books that would soon find their way from the Old Country.

To what extent the written music collections arrived before 1940 is not clear. But one figure who was significant in promoting the use of the Old Country music books was fiddler/composer Dan R. MacDonald. While in Scotland during World War Two, Dan R. discovered some of these music books and sent several home to friends in Cape Breton – Dan Hugh MacEachern and Alex Francis MacKay in particular, as both were committed to reading the music and sharing the tunes in their respective communities. Eventually, these same books and the many others that had followed from the Golden Age caught Buddy's interest and thus began his journey to acquire his massive repertoire, which stands out today as one of the most comprehensive repertoires being performed by a Scottish fiddler anywhere in the world.

Jody Stecher in *Strings* shares the following observation: "Buddy is continually expanding his repertoire and has introduced many new tunes to other Cape Breton players ... Like many other Cape Breton fiddlers, Buddy learns many of his tunes from printed sources ... He had ample time [while a CNR stationmaster] to pore over great Scottish tune books of past centuries such as the Kerr's, Lowe's, Kohler's, and the Athol and Skye collections. ... 'Book tunes' such as Scott Skinner's compositions ... tunes newly composed by young Cape Breton players, old traditional reels with no names at all, perhaps with Gaelic words that only the old remember, an occasional Irish or Shetland reel, or one of his cousin's Dan Rory MacDonald's 2,000 compositions – Buddy plays them all ... In this literature but aural tradition, the page is a handy and much-used storage and retrieval medium. It is respected but never dictates style or expression."

Stecher continues by describing Buddy's capacity to perform this seamless repository of tunes. "Strathspeys follow marches and are tension builders. They give way to faster strathspeys that segue into reels. With the reels comes release and flight. A-major tunes, A-minor tunes, modal tunes with no third at all, straying no further than a side trip to C-major, with the transition so smooth that you hardly notice. As each reel flows into the next the intensity of the music is increased again, and as Buddy really gets rolling he begins to play the reels only once each. He seems to sit further back in his chair with each tune, and his eyes see less and less ... One foot is tapping heel to toe, the other flat on the sole. His elbow is dripping perspiration. Now at his musical height, the whole notion of tune has gone out the window. The linear progression has been transformed into ecstatic flow of melody . . ."

In terms of Buddy's Scottish-Cape Breton repertoire, it has as much to do with the tunes that were published in early Scotland. James Hunter explains that the 1734 *Drummond Castle Manuscript* has the earliest written records of tunes like "*Tullochgorum*" and "*Caber Feidh*" – both tunes are part of Buddy's repertoire.

As for Buddy's style, it has everything to do with the fact he has been entrenched among the *Gàidhealtach* – including Gaelic-speaking fiddlers as well as the old-time pipers. Kimberley Fraser, a young celebrated Cape Breton fiddler, has given recent talks in Scotland at the Elphinstone Institute, University of Aberdeen, and in Massachusetts' Boston College on the links between the piping tradition and the music of fiddlers like Buddy.

She observes, "Buddy developed his technique of playing during the time when Gaelic-style bagpipe music still functioned as dance music in Cape Breton's Gaelic community. His music is a prime example of the significant role bagpipes played in shaping Cape Breton's fiddling tradition. A variety of pipe-style characteristics, including complex grace notes, four-note cuts, drones, and 'neutral notes' (corresponding to the 'in-between' pitches on the pipe chanter), are entrenched in his music. Like most other fiddlers of his generation, Buddy often turned to pipe books when selecting tunes for his repertoire. Particularly notable is his selection of pipe marches and the extraordinary way in which he expresses them. Through his bowing and left hand embellishments, Buddy phrases the march in such a way that highlights the important pulses of the tune.

"The piping influence is especially evident in Buddy's version of the Scottish favourite, 'Miss MacLeod's Reel.' In 19th century Scottish publications such as the *Skye* and *Athol Collections*, this tune is published with $F^\#$ (F sharp) as the focal point of the 7th bars in both the first and second turns. This is the most common Cape Breton setting. However, Buddy plays a G natural as the focal point in these bars, putting that portion of the melody in the mode of A mixolydian. This is an A major scale with a flat 7, the same scale as the pipe chanter. Buddy also adds G natural passing tones to the 1st and 3rd bars of the first turn. It is important to note that Buddy does not play these G notes fully 'natural', but rather as more of a neutral tone between G natural and G sharp. This is a stylistic feature of the older fiddlers and can be linked to the ambiguous quality of that note on the pipe chanter. It is uncertain where Buddy learned his version of this tune; however, it is interesting to note that a similar setting can be found in the 19th century publication, *The Caledonian Repository of Music* (reissued as *William Gunn's Collection of Pipe Music*)."

Buddy was immersed in the two worlds of the aural and written traditions that focus on the fiddling, piping, Gaelic song and dance traditions. It is this blend that has shaped his music. But would that exciting tradition he experienced remain?

By 1965, rural Cape Breton area was feeling some sense of decline in the music despite the fact that the home sessions and outdoor concerts, mainstays in the music tradition, were on the rise. The local dance scene, however, another important feature in sustaining the tradition, was beginning to wane except when Cape Bretoners returned home annually for the summer holidays. This made summer a time to renew the music and dancing especially. For some, the thoughts of a decline in the music were rather incongruent with what was still happening among diehard music enthusiasts where Cape Bretoners gathered – home and away.

Throughout the 1940s, 1950s and 1960s, dances with Cape Breton fiddlers were popular in Boston, Detroit and Toronto as well as Cape Breton. The local radio stations such as CJFX in Antigonish and CJCB in Sydney played the music. Radio productions in Sydney at the time featured artists like Tina Campbell, Joe MacLean, Bill Lamey and Dan Joe MacInnis. All these fiddlers took turns hosting their own programs on CJCB Radio. In addition to regular radio appearances, Winston Fitzgerald was a dominant performer on CJCB-TV in Sydney. But all came to a stop by the mid-1960s. Although CBC television in Halifax was going strong with *Don Messer's Jubilee*, the program, which was carried regionally and remained so until 1969, did very little to host the music of the Cape Breton fiddler. Guest appearances by some Cape Breton fiddlers did take place, however.

Among the Cape Breton fiddlers, the history of the commercial recording tradition is most interesting with a series of ups and downs over many years. By the mid-1960s, the idea of the fiddlers continuing to record their music on vinyl was on hold. Despite the fiddlers' reluctance to record, the recording companies reissued, onto vinyl, the early recordings that were on the old 78 format, and many original vinyl albums were reissued as compilations/collectors' items.

Inverness County native and celebrated fiddler Alex Gillis left Cape Breton in 1922 and subsequently settled in Boston. He formed The Inverness Serenaders who recorded on the old 78 format with Decca. This was a significant development for the music of the Cape Breton fiddler. In 1934, three legendary Cape Breton fiddlers, Dan J. Campbell, Angus Allan Gillis and Angus Chisholm, made their way to Montreal to record several 78s on the Celtic label. They, too, "set a benchmark of quality and timing that continues to be reflected in the recording of today's great fiddlers." Frank Macdonald of *The Inverness Oran* further writes, "By the end of the 20th century, Inverness County musicians were recording enough music to fill a library ..."

Buddy says, "I used to listen to some of the old recordings. I'd pick up the odd tune that was played by Angus Chisholm or Little Jack [MacDonald] on those records. They were good. To hear them on the records was nice. I'd hear them on CJFX Radio. But I never felt a strong urge to record myself. I just never felt that I was ready."

Buddy was not part of this early effort in radio or television. He recalls, "I was always busy at work at the CN. Then I was playing at dances. So, I felt I was pretty busy doing my own thing ... I really never took the time to think whether I wanted to be part of that. It was nice and I know that the people appreciated the TV and radio.

"Now in these parts [Inverness County] the only media we had to do that was CJFX. They seemed to have an interest in the music. I made many tapes for CJFX in the early years. They would record my music at the studio and at different concerts in the local area. That was nice. It was not a money thing. I know that the people enjoyed hearing the music so that was all that mattered. I guess I got started at that serious recording stuff with CBC in the early 1970s when John Allan [Cameron] asked me to play on CBC. They wanted to do something with the Cape Breton music for a change."

Buddy did, however, have an association with the studio scene for several decades prior to his CBC work in Halifax. In addition to his field recordings with CJFX, CJCB-TV in Sydney hosted Buddy in the early 1950s for a special guest appearance. When he visited Boston in the '60s and '70s, his music was recorded for radio stations in Boston. During his visits to Scotland, beginning in 1970, BBC recorded his music for radio and again in subsequent years on several occasions. He made several recordings with CBC Radio in Sydney and Halifax that received local and national broadcasts. He recorded with the Cape Breton Symphony after joining them in 1979.

Buddy performs on several other recordings with high profile musicians. He is featured on the CBC recording *Atlantic Fiddling* (1979), and on the Lismore recording *Down Home* (1986), which highlights the fiddle music of Scotland, the U.S. and Canada. Buddy was recorded at Island Studio, Cape Breton, in 1995, for a compilation of music from the Gaelic tradition. Beginning in 1992, he was featured in a series of videos produced by SeaBright Productions: *Master Cape Breton Fiddler – Buddy MacMaster*; *In Concert, Buddy MacMaster;* and more recently a DVD titled, *The Best of Buddy MacMaster*. Celtic Colours International Festival released a series of CD recordings that featured Buddy's music, among others, beginning in 1997 for worldwide distribution.

Buddy explains that several companies had approached him in the 1950s to do a solo recording. He would respond by saying that he felt he was not ready. He would further explain that he was involved in other things with his music. In 1989, however, Buddy, at the age of sixty-five did release his first solo recording. It was produced with the utmost care and attention by Allister MacGillivray and recorded at a professional studio in Toronto. The recording was a result of an invitation from Father Greg MacLeod at Cape Breton University who asked Buddy to record for the archives at the Beaton Institute. This material was later released as a commercial recording – *Judique on the Floor*. It is often characterized as Buddy's best in a studio setting.

Buddy's second solo recording, *Glencoe Hall*, appeared in 1991; his third, *The Judique Flyer*, in 2000; and a fourth, *Buddy MacMaster – Cape Breton Tradition*, in 2003. In 2005, he teamed up with his niece Natalie MacMaster to record *Natalie and Buddy MacMaster*.

This wealth of recorded material ensures people will be enjoying and learning for years to come and this will help continue Buddy's legacy.

One benchmark for the revival era was the highly acclaimed 1971 CBC-TV production *The Vanishing Cape Breton Fiddler,* produced by Ron MacInnis. It had become the talk of the town. It did generate some discussion among those who were strong proponents of the need to keep the music tradition alive and well for generations to follow. How could this music be disappearing, many asked?

In fact, there was every reason to be concerned, not so much with the excitement being felt by those who could regularly hear busy fiddlers like Buddy, but rather by those who wondered whether the next generation would actually be as interested in playing the fiddle – learning the tunes through books and keeping in contact with the local mentors to ensure that the tunes were being played in the old tradition. This was the real concern.

So entered a revival in the Cape Breton Scottish heritage – a heritage that had persisted in rural Cape Breton for two hundred years but was now being challenged. The Gaelic Society of Cape Breton was established in 1969 to preserve the Gaelic language. Chapters were established across Cape Breton. As mentioned earlier, the Cape Breton Fiddlers' Association was formed in 1972. Activists were now being prepared to rekindle an interest in the Gaelic language and the traditional music. In 1974, the idea of the fiddlers going back into recording commercially was further entrenched through the work of Mark Wilson of Rounder Records. He engaged the local fiddlers to enter a new era of recording – one that would give the fiddler a greater sense of control of the process. Thus began the post-1970 era, a new effort to nurture the music, the language, the dance and new opportunities to collect, publish and preserve the music of the Cape Breton fiddler. The era would embark on a journey of discovery, innovation and subtle initiatives to challenge the old tradition and embrace the new one.

In the centre of all this was Buddy MacMaster and he would remain steadfast to the tradition. In 1992, Jody Stecher wrote, "[H]e has steered a middle course, resisting all new stylistic trends but, interestingly, not resisting new tunes."

Subsequently, throughout the 1970s, 1980s, the 1990s and into the new millennium, Buddy's music was to become recognized internationally by fiddle and folk music enthusiasts whether they were in Scotland, the United States or other parts of Canada. Buddy would now be part of a new era of revivalism. Now the Cape Breton fiddler was to become part of that revivalism, making sure that the next generation would prevail.

Buddy had a direct link with the early Scottish music that had been published in the Old Country. He had a direct line with the community of Cape Breton fiddlers and other tradition bearers as they rendered the tunes, the songs and the dancing in the old tradition for the enjoyment of the Gaels internationally. He continues to enjoy the immense interest of those who have come to appreciate the Celtic music of post-1970. Buddy MacMaster's direct link with the music is as up close and personal as it is unique and far-reaching.

Accolades

In the July 10, 1991, issue of *The Reporter* Frances MacEachen writes, "You do not talk to Buddy about his excellence as a fiddler or proof of his generosity to Cape Breton and beyond." In interviews, Buddy's behaviour is consistent with this fact. He simply shies away from any discussion that focuses on him, the person. He'll always find a way to change the subject.

MacEachen adds, "In this sense, he is often difficult to interview." And many are the interviews he has given over the years – local writers, travelling journalists, media personnel and academics from many disciplines have approached Buddy for interviews. On such occasions, he is often asked about being an effective role model for youth. Generally, his response is always the same. He'll reflect on the idea for a moment. Privately, he will think about an earlier era. He'll think about behaviour he displayed while he was a younger musician – a free spirit. He'll recall the occasions when the temptation to accept a dram was difficult to resist – and so he didn't resist. This was coupled with the style of the times, the late nights in music, his longstanding popularity and the desire to perform "at the drop of a hat." With these thoughts, he would question aloud whether he was a good role model. But all those who knew him then, as they know him now, convey the same message. "Buddy was never out of sorts. He always had a gentle, quiet and calm manner about him. Buddy was always ... Buddy."

Buddy recognizes today that he has become more settled. He married late and began a family. In his modest way, he now recognizes that he does have something to offer and is a role model. He is satisfied that as he projects his own personal values as reflected in his love and respect for his faith, family, community and music – in that order – there is something there for others to consider.

In 1982, Dr. Ora McManus, former Director of Continuing Education at Cape Breton University recognized that the Cape Breton Celtic music tradition was in an era of revivalism and that exciting things would soon emerge for the music. In November of that year, he promoted a special ceilidh honouring Buddy MacMaster to elevate the importance of the Celtic music generally, and it was the first of many and deserving tributes to come for Buddy for the next twenty-five years.

As part of this special ceilidh, a liturgy introduced the occasion. Later, a banquet was held where the then Premier of the Province of Nova Scotia, John M. Buchanan, addressed the gathering. Guest musicians from across Cape Breton performed. In addition, the evening included people from all walks of life expressing words of gratitude. Gifts were presented from many organizations, societies, groups and agencies wanting to pay their respect to Buddy. Dr. Charles MacDonald, of the Department of Humanities and Religious Studies at Cape Breton University, introduced the guest speaker, Rev. Malcolm MacDonell, past president of St. Francis Xavier University.

Rev. MacDonell said, "One of the most distinguished artists in this distinctive cultural expression is Hugh Allan MacMaster. He is a gentleman in whom we find this cultural artistry deeply rooted in an exemplary Christian character. He is a man with a responsible sense of citizenship, as witnessed in his years in municipal council and our school board, not to mention the many other services he performs for our community. When you blend character and culture and citizenship and categorize them together with generosity, happy the community adored and served by such a person."

A few days later, the Antigonish newspaper *The Casket* reported, "Dr.

McManus spoke to the role that Buddy had played in the revival of the Scottish music tradition and praised Buddy for his tireless effort to expose the Cape Breton music to an ever-growing audience at home and abroad." *The Casket* added, "The Master of Ceremonies, Norman MacDonald, Professor of Celtic Studies at UCCB [now Cape Breton University], handled the hectic task of introductions in Gaelic wit ... and also read out messages from people like the Honorable Allan J. MacEachen, Scottish fiddlers Donald Riddle and Tom Anderson, and Cape Breton (fiddler) Bill Lamey."

Perhaps one of the more heartfelt expressions of gratitude to Buddy occurred in the summer of 1990 when the community of Glencoe Mills hosted an evening of food, music and frolic, as well as the liturgy for the MacMaster family. Donald Angus Campbell, a parish representative, spoke on behalf of the people of Glencoe Mills. His speech, as quoted, in part, by Frances MacEachen in *The Reporter*, brought listeners back to an earlier Glencoe Mills.

"There were people and there was production ... And there was music ... But times have changed ... We don't have our violinists, but we do have our church, our hall and our cemetery ... We are proud of them and we do have ourselves ... There are very few people about whom you can say, 'He really makes a difference!' The difference between our parish living and our parish dying is Buddy MacMaster."

In 1998, two special ceilidhs were organized to honour Buddy. In March, he shared the spotlight with renowned pianist Elizabeth Beaton of Mabou and outstanding traditional step dancer from Deepdale, Willie Fraser. Frank Macdonald of *The Inverness Oran* wrote, "... a few brief moments reminded people once again of the spirit that has sustained Cape Breton's culture through economic despair, population depletion, and global influences."

In November, the Celtic Colours International Festival hosted a ceilidh for Buddy in Judique. Two renowned musicians who attended were quoted in *The Inverness Oran*. David Greenberg of Maryland, U.S., who now resides in Halifax, said upon first hearing Buddy's music, "It

St. Francis Xavier University presented Buddy with an honorary degree in 1995.

Governor-General Adrienne Clarkson invests Buddy into the Order of Canada at a ceremony in Ottawa, February 28, 2001. (CP Photo/Tom Hanson)

Buddy signs The Order of Nova Scotia Official Book of Records after his induction into the order in 2003. In the background are Lieutenant-Governor Myra Freeman and her husband Lawrence A. Freeman. (Shirley Robb/Communications Nova Scotia photo)

Buddy acknowledging his honorary degree from Cape Breton University, at a special convocation held in St. Andrew's Church in Judique, 2006.

Buddy and Marie MacMaster enjoy a rare quiet moment during Judique's celebration of Buddy's eightieth birthday, 2004.

changed my musical direction." Greenberg is a classically trained violinist and he has mastered the old style music of Cape Breton. Scottish violinist Alasdair Fraser said, "[Buddy] showed me a way to put the dirt and hair and haggis back into the tunes again."

Frank Macdonald describes Natalie MacMaster's observation of the huge turnout. She said, "They came from around the world because they had heard his music, but they came from across Cape Breton because they knew him as a neighbour and a friend, as a man modest and humble about his gifts, prepared to share them for the benefit of the community and the world."

Also attending was Warden A.J. MacDougall, who referred to Buddy as "the master" and said, "In the hands of some, it [the fiddle] can be a weapon ... some wood, some steel strings, some horse hair. You have to wonder how it is even possible to get it to turn out music. It is through the master's hands that happens, and there is no better way than through the hand of the master."

In October 2004, the community of Judique paid tribute to Buddy on the occasion of his eightieth birthday, just as they did in 1994 for his seventieth birthday. It was a wonderful evening of family and friends. The M.C. for the evening, Bobby MacEachern of CIGO Radio, Port Hawkesbury, addressed the gathering with many words of esteem for Buddy. The gala event focused on Buddy's family and close friends. Many had come from far and near to participate in the event. The evening began with a celebration of the liturgy at St. Andrew's Church. Later in the Judique hall, a banquet followed with entertainment, presentations and many sentiments expressing gratitude for Buddy's talent and generosity.

Two distinguished universities in Nova Scotia have honoured Buddy. In April 1995, Buddy received an honorary degree from St. Francis Xavier University, Antigonish. Dr. Sean Riley, President, presided at the convocation. A university official stated, "This fiddling master has become a force in Eastern Nova Scotia Celtic culture, not only as a teacher but as a mentor for the younger audience as well ... His contribution to the retention of the Celtic culture and his generosity in performing for charitable fundraisers are two of many good reasons to recommend Buddy MacMaster for an honorary degree."

Cape Breton University granted him an honorary degree in October 2006. The university president, Dr. John Harker, presided. Dr. Richard MacKinnon, Tier 1 Canada Research Chair in Intangible Cultural Heritage and Director for the Centre of Cape Breton Studies at Cape Breton University, read the citation describing Buddy's excellent contribution and service to the music and cultural community of Cape Breton. He emphasized Buddy's role as an iconic treasure in the cultural mix of Canada. On this occasion, Rodney MacDonald, Premier of Nova Scotia, spoke. He said, "It is fitting tonight that Cape Breton University recognizes the *master* for he has been a true ambassador for his island and his province. It is a reflection of Cape Breton University's commitment to education both within its walls and to the broader community."

Premier Rodney, a noted fiddler and dancer himself, stepped outside his official script to reminisce: "Driving up through Mabou Ridge, we soon headed down the gravel road for the dance in Glencoe – and then we saw the light [everyone sees the light] and could hear the sweet sound of one of Buddy's famous jigs and the feet on the floor – we'd dance all night!"

In recent years, the music industry acknowledged Buddy. In February 2006, the East Coast Music Awards presented him with the Dr. Helen Creighton Lifetime Achievement Award and he received three standing ovations from the full house.

In 2006, Buddy was nominated for the prestigious U.S. Folk Alliance Elaine Weissman Lifetime Achievement Award, in the category of Living Performer. He is the only Canadian who was short-listed.

In December 2006, Buddy was the first performer from outside the United Kingdom to be inducted into the Scottish Traditional Music Hall of Fame. The award is given to musicians who have been in the industry for over thirty years and have contributed significantly to the music. Another inductee is Paddy Maloney of The Chieftains.

The Governments of Canada and Nova Scotia have recognized Buddy MacMaster. In 1993, Buddy received the Canada Medal, an award to celebrate special Canadian personalities while commemorating the 125th anniversary of the founding of Canada. In 2000, Buddy was named a Member of the Order of Canada in recognition of a lifetime of distinguished service in music. Presented with the award by the Governor-General at the investiture ceremony in 2001, the citation read, in part, "As an ambassador of Canadian music and a mentor to many, he is leading a Gaelic renaissance in Canada and abroad." He was honoured with the Order of Nova Scotia in 2003 for his outstanding contribution to the Celtic culture and community.

Danny Graham is the former vice-chair of the board for the Celtic Music Interpretative Centre in Judique. He recounts a story that reflects the respect for Buddy's support to the Centre and to the music generally. The board had decided that the new building, which opened in 2006, would have Buddy MacMaster perform the first tune to be played on the fiddle in the building. The planning was still in the works when a group from the local tourist bureau arrived to see what the centre had to offer. It was a rather spontaneous visit. The staff was very welcoming to the visitors. At one point it was suggested that Kinnon Beaton, a celebrated fiddler and manager of the centre, play a few tunes. Danny explains, "In order to preserve this first-tune occasion with Buddy, Kinnon decided that he would take the fiddle outside the building to play his music." In 2006, the Celtic Music Interpretive Centre established the Buddy MacMaster School of Fiddling.

Francene Gillis best depicts the meaning of the tributes that have been paid to Buddy MacMaster in his lifetime. "Indeed Buddy MacMaster has brought much to many through his gentle, heartfelt giving of music. As we pass through this lifetime, a goal many of us have is to have touched one life or to have made a difference. Buddy MacMaster through his living (and) what his music expresses has done that time and time again."

As a Cape Breton fiddler, Buddy MacMaster is a gifted musician. He was raised in a community of musicians who understood the old tradition of learning and sharing music. In his youth, he came to know this through local fiddlers who would visit his home, like Ronald Mac-Donnell, Alexander MacDonnell and especially Angus MacMaster. Buddy lived in the company of many excellent fiddlers from the wider Cape Breton community who also understood the need to share, including two great composers – Dan R. MacDonald and Dan Hughie MacEachern. He knew Little Jack MacDonald, Angus Chisholm, Mary MacDonald and Bill Lamey – all were giants in the music and all were extremely influential in shaping his musical interest and talent at a very young age. He learned early in his playing career the importance of reading the music and encouraged others to follow this tradition. He applied the written note to perfection. He compiled a significant collection of great books from the United Kingdom, the U.S. and Canada. In addition to local compositions, he plays the music of Gow, Marshall and Skinner among others. His repertoire is immense. He plays all – jigs, reels, strathspeys, clogs, hornpipes, marches and pastoral airs. There is seemingly no end to the tunes he can render. In recognition of his craft, Buddy has had many tunes written in his honour.

Buddy developed into a great dance player especially. He spent countless hours performing in his native Inverness County at dance halls in Mabou, Judique, Inverness, Deepdale, Glencoe and Strathlorne, to name a few. He was in demand constantly for dances throughout other parts of Cape Breton as well. Buddy can be at his kitchen table in the morning playing and learning new tunes. Later that same morning he can be at a church playing at a funeral and still later in the afternoon at a local wedding. He could then prepare for an early concert appearance and then make his way to perform at a three-hour dance. In fact, he has. Buddy makes his talent as a player available to all who will listen. He expects very little in return for his gift of music to so many.

Buddy MacMaster is as popular a person as he is a musician. Kind and considerate, he helps those who are in need in ways unknown to many. Throughout his lifetime, he has demonstrated that he understands the value and importance of sharing. He developed a keen awareness of the importance of good citizenship as portrayed through his work in municipal government. He has a great sense of humour and a very dry wit. He is loyal and tolerant of those with little or no ambition or talent. He is a humble person. He perseveres at learning new tunes, in performing well, and in helping and caring for neighbours, friends, family, or a special cause or special event. He is a person of deep pride. He loves his Judique and Little Judique too, his Cape Breton, his heritage, his music and most importantly his family. He is strong-willed. He is a determined competitor. He competes with himself constantly, trying to improve his music and his character so they will be better tomorrow than they are today – that is a tall order to which Buddy MacMaster aspires. And yet, he does that very well, too.

Linden MacIntyre warmly describes Buddy MacMaster: "In Buddy, humanity, integrity, a great talent, and a remarkable fidelity to history have transformed a rich local heritage into a universal genre."

Buddy, however, modestly says, "I'm just Buddy."

Chronology

1798 The MacDonalds, Buddy's mother's people, arrive at Judique Banks from Scotland

1800 (Early) The MacMasters (Buddy's father's people) arrive from Scotland

1888-1970 John Duncan MacMaster is born/died

1900-1986 Sarah Agnes Macdonald is born/died

1923 The MacMaster family moves to Timmins, Ontario

1924 Hugh Allan "Buddy" MacMaster is born

1929 The MacMaster family returns to Judique

1933 Meets composer Dan Hughie MacEachern at a picnic in Judique

1935 First public performance (Port Hood Amateur Hour)

1939 Receives his first pay for a dance (Troy School)

1940 Dan R. MacDonald leaves for overseas (Second World War)

1941 Dan R. sends a supply of music books to Dan Hughie MacEachern and Alex Francis MacKay

1941 Gordon MacQuarrie releases *Cape Breton Scottish Melodies Collection*

1943 Buddy starts work at Canadian National (CN)

1943 CJFX Radio goes on air in Antigonish

1948 Takes his first and only music lesson visit with Mildred Leadbeater

1948 Purchases his first music book – *The Scottish Violinist*

1949 Begins a regular dance circuit in Inverness area

1953 Appears on CJCB-TV Sydney (Grand Opening)

1953 Plays dances at the famous Neilly's Hall, Inverness County

1957 Performs at the first Broad Cove Scottish Concert

1965 New hall opens in Glendale, which becomes a regular dance venue for Buddy

1965 Begins to play at the Glencoe dances

1968 Sworn in as an elected councillor for Judique district

1968 Buddy and Marie Beaton marry

1970 Dan R. MacDonald composes and dedicates the "Glencoe March" to Buddy

1970 His first trip to Scotland where he appears at the Oban Mod

1971 The CBC documentary *The Vanishing Cape Breton Fiddler* is released

1972 Joins *Ceilidh* (taped in Halifax for CBC national TV)

1973 Cape Breton Festival of Scottish Fiddling is staged for the first time

1973 CBC *Ceilidh* goes to air

1975 Leaves County Council

1975 Goes to Scotland to participate in the First Official Ceilidh at Edinburgh Castle

1976 Dan R. MacDonald dies

1979 Joins Cape Breton Symphony (on tour in Vancouver)

1979 Performs on the first live transatlantic ceilidh, a joint CBC/BBC production

1979 Tours Scotland with Cape Breton musicians

1982 Cape Breton University presents a tribute ceilidh to Buddy MacMaster with an island-wide turnout

1984 Participates in the Port Townsend American Fiddle Tunes Camp, Washington

1984 Participates in the Cape Breton University-sponsored concert series recorded by CBC

1984 Performs at sell-out concert at Queen's Hall, Edinburgh, Scotland, with Cape Breton Symphony

1985 Participates in the California Traditional Music Society Summer Solstice Festival, Los Angeles

1985 Purchased a violin made by Sergio Peresson, of which he is most proud

1986 First teaching session at Valley of the Moon Scottish Fiddling School, California

1986 Buddy participates in the Bluemont Concert series in West Virginia

1987 Appears at the Augusta Heritage Arts Workshops in Elkins, West Virginia

1987 Performs in folk festival in Philadelphia

1988 Retires from Canadian National (CN)

1988 Participates in the Scottish Fiddle Rally Weekend in Boston

1989 Releases first solo recording – *Judique on the Floor*

1990 Glencoe Mills community honours Buddy in a tribute ceilidh

1991 Releases second solo recording – *Glencoe Hall*

1992 SeaBright Productions releases video *Master Cape Breton Fiddler – Buddy MacMaster*

1992 Begins teaching at Sablah Mòr Ostaig, Skye, Scotland

1992 Participates in the annual University of Chicago Folk Festival

1993 Performs at University College, Cork, Ireland, Festival of Traditional Music

1993 Receives the Canada Medal (issued on the 125th anniversary of the founding of Canada)

1994 Performs with the Strathspey and Reel Society of New Hampshire

1995 Appears at the 19th Annual Washington Irish Folk Festival

1995 Buddy receives an honourary doctoral degree from St. Francis Xavier University

1995 Mary Elizabeth MacMaster, Buddy's daughter, graduates from St. Francis Xavier University

1996 Allan Gerard MacMaster, Buddy's son, graduates from St. Francis Xavier University

1996 Ceilidh Trail School of Celtic Music opens (Buddy instructs)

1996 Dan Hughie MacEachern dies

1997 Plays U.S. national anthem at Boston Red Sox and Detroit Tigers baseball game

1997 Performs at the Rockport Folk Festival in Maine

1999 Appears at the Annual Cowboy Poetry Gathering in Elko, Nevada

1999 Participates at the Celtic Sundance Festival, Utah

2000 Awarded the Order of Canada

2000 Releases his third solo recording – *The Judique Flyer*

2001 Participates in the Rocky Mountain Fiddle Camp, Denver, Colorado

2003 Receives the Order of Nova Scotia

2003 Releases his fourth solo recording – *Buddy MacMaster - Cape Breton Tradition*

2006 Receives Dr. Helen Creighton Lifetime Achievement Award at the ECMAs – the East Coast Music Awards

2005 Records with his niece Natalie MacMaster – *Natalie and Buddy MacMaster*

2006 Buddy MacMaster's School of Scottish Fiddling opens at the Celtic Music Interpretative Centre, Judique

2006 Appears at the 50th annual Broad Cove Scottish Concert

2006 Receives an honorary doctorate degree from Cape Breton University

2006 Inducted into the Scottish Traditional Music Hall of Fame – the first person from outside the United Kingdom to be inducted

2007 Nominated Folk Alliance Elaine Weissman Lifetime Achievement Award

2007 Performs with niece Natalie MacMaster on a special BBC-TV series recorded in Judique

References

Addison, Emily. "The Perception and Value of Dance Halls in Inverness County, Cape Breton." Honours Thesis. Trent University Geography Department. April 2001.

Arsenault, Gabe. (Interview). 20 November 2006. Boston, USA.

Beaton, Joey. "Dance Music – Buddy MacMaster and Donald Angus Beaton [Tune Titles]. Unpublished Document. Mabou. 1997.

Beaton, Joey. Interview with Bobby MacEachern. CIGO Radio – 101.5 The Hawk, Port Hawkesbury. July 2000.

Beaton, Kay. (Interview). September 2006. Halifax, NS.

Beaton, Sarah. (Conversation). July 2006. Mabou, NS.

Best, Harold M. *Music Through The Eyes of Faith*. New York: Harper San Francisco, 1993.

Blaustein, Richard. "Rethinking Folk Revivalism: Grass-Roots Preservationism and Folk Romanticism." *Transforming Tradition. Folk Music Revivals Examined*. Ed. Neil V. Rosenberg. Chicago: University of Illinois Press, 1993: 267.

Borcherding, Bob. "Augusta Heritage Workshop – Scottish Cape Breton Week." *Scottish Fiddling Revival Newsletter*. The U.S. National Scottish Fiddling Association.

"Buddy MacMaster Broadcast Dates and Programmes – Canada-wide." CBC Radio-Canada ERN Radio Archives Search: 309 PLGPRO Documents. Retrieved 18 August 2006, Halifax, NS.

Buddy MacMaster Ceilidh Tribute. Technician Cyril MacInnis. Audiotape. AVTC Complex, Sydney, NS. 11 November 1982.

Cameron, John Donald. (Conversation). June 2006. Port Hawkesbury, NS.

Cameron, John Donald. (Interview).15 July 2006. Port Hawkesbury, NS.

Cameron, John Donald. "Moxham's Castle." *Am Braighe* Summer 1997: 7.

Campbell, A.D., and R.A. MacLean. *Beyond the Atlantic Roar: A Study of the Nova Scotia Scot.* Toronto: McClelland and Stewart, 1974.

Campbell, John. "Fiddle Festival at Gaelic College Celebrates our Musical Heritage." *Cape Breton Post* 18 Aug. 1990: 15.

Campbell, John and Sandy Campbell, et al. Editors. "Gaelic Society Looks to Expanding Membership." *The Cape Breton Highlander* 9 April 1969.

Campbell, John and Sandy Campbell, et al. Editors. "Big Bash Set For Broad Cove." *The Cape Breton Highlander* 19 July 1967: 3.

Campbell, John and Sandy Campbell, et al. Editors. "At Inverness – Ceilidh Opens Thursday." *The Cape Breton Highlander* 17 July 1966.

Campbell, John and Sandy Campbell, et al. Editors. "CBC Ceilidh Series to Begin Thurs., May 16." *The Cape Breton Highlander*. 4 May 1974: 4.

Campbell, John and Sandy Campbell, et al. Editors. "The Scotch Concert! Closest Thing to The Newport Festival This Side of Rhode Island." *The Cape Breton Highlander* 23 July 1996:10.

Campbell, John and Sandy Campbell, et al. Editors. "Judique on The Floor..." *The Cape Breton Highlander* 10 July 1968: 18.

Campbell, John and Sandy Campbell, et al. Editors. "Johnstown Milling Frolic a Must for Tourist and Native." *The Cape Breton Highlander* 23 August 1997.

Campbell, John and Sandy Campbell, et al. Editors. "Down-east Gathering Big Draw in Boston." *The Cape Breton Highlander* 19 June 1968: 19.

Campbell, John and Sandy Campbell, et al. Editors. "Highland Village Day Scheduled for Aug. 3." *The Cape Breton Highlander* 5 July 1968.

Campbell, John Lorne. "Highland Links with Nova Scotia." *Scots Magazine*. Oct. 1953.

"Canadian Gaels A Hit." *Oban Times*. 8 Nov. 1979.

"Cape Breton Fiddlers (5th in Series) – Buddy MacMaster." *Scotia Sun* 1972-1973 Series.

Cape Breton Symphony. *Cape Breton Symphony – Fiddle Volume I*. Record Album. Brampton, ON: Brownrigg Productions.

Cape Breton Symphony. *Cape Breton Symphony – Fiddle*. Record Album. Toronto, ON: Recorded at Sounds Interchange.

Celtic Music Interpretative Centre – The Gateway to Celtic Music. Brochure for public distribution. 2006.

Chisholm, Archie Neil. Interview. CBC Halifax Archive: Tape #P-3494. 1992.

Conners, Chris. "Buddy MacMaster Given Lifetime Award." *Cape Breton Post* 28 Feb. 2006: A1.

Cooke Peter. *The Fiddle Tradition of the Shetland Isles*. Great Britain: Cambridge University Press, 1986.

Doherty, Elizabeth A., Ireland. E-mail to the author. February 2007.

Doherty, Elizabeth A. *The Music of Cape Breton – An Irish Perspective*. Cork, Ireland: The Traditional Music Archive/The Irish Traditional Music Society, University College, 1994.

Doherty, Elizabeth A. *The Paradox of the Periphery, Evolution of the Cape Breton Fiddle Tradition 1928-1995*. Ph.D. Diss. University of Limerick, 1996.

Doherty, Elizabeth A. *Traditional Music from Cape Breton Island*. CD Booklet. Nimbus Records Ltd., UK and USA, 1993.

Donovan, Ken, ed. *The Island: New Perspectives on Cape Breton's History*. Sydney: University College of Cape Breton Press, 1990.

Ducharme, Mary Anne. *Archie Neil – A Triumph of a Life!* Breton Books: Sydney, Nova Scotia 1992.

Ducharme, Mary Anne. "Creignish Fiddlers: Interview with Frank MacInnis." *Partici-Paper* January/February 1997: 3.

Dunlay, Kate. "A Cape Breton Primer; Canada's Old World Music." *Sing Out!* Fall 1989: 4.

Dunlay, Kate. *Traditional Celtic Violin Music of Cape Breton*. Toronto: DunGreen Music, 1996.

Dunlay, Kate and D.L. Reich. *Traditional Celtic Fiddle Music of Cape Breton*. New Hampshire: Fiddlecase Books, 1986.

Dunn, Charles W. *Highland Settler: A Portrait of the Scottish Gael in Nova Scotia*. Toronto: University of Toronto Press, 1953.

Dunn, Jacqueline A. "The Sound of Gaelic is in the Fiddler's Music." Senior Essay St. Francis Xavier University, 1991.

Feintuch, Burt. Liner Notes. *Buddy MacMaster – Cape Breton Tradition*. Rounder Records Corp., 2003.

Fraser, Kimberley. E-mail to the author. December 2006.

Fraser, Simon (Captain). *The Airs and Melodies Peculiar to the Highlands of Scotland and The Isles*. Sydney, NS: Paul S. Cranford, 1982.

Frew, Chris. "Travels with a Fiddle." *West Highland Free Press* 31 Jan. 1986.

Garrison, Virginia Hope. *Traditional and Non-Traditional Teaching and Learning Practices in Folk Music. An Ethnographic Field Study of Cape Breton Fiddling*. Ph.D. Diss. University of Wisconsin, 1985: 157-158.

Gibson, John. *Traditional Gaelic Piping 1745-1945*. Montreal: McGill-Queen's Press, 1998.

Gillis, Francene. "A Visit with Buddy MacMaster." *The Inverness Oran* 26 Aug. 1992: 8-9.

Gillis, Rannie. "MacMaster the Dean of Cape Breton Fiddlers." *Cape Breton Post* 28 Feb. 2001: 3.

Graham, Danny. (Interview). August 2006. Judique, NS.

Graham, Glenn. *The Cape Breton Fiddle: Making and Maintaining Tradition*. Sydney, NS: Cape Breton University Press, 2006.

Grant, Laura Jean. "Great Scot! Buddy MacMaster inducted into Scottish Traditional Music Hall of Fame." *Cape Breton Post* 15 Dec. 2006.

Guest, Bill. *Canadian Fiddlers*. Nova Scotia: Lancelot Press, 1985.

Harvey, Daniel C. "Scottish Immigration to Cape Breton." *Dalhousie Review* 22 (1941): 313- 324.

Howarth, John. E-mail to Marlene MacInnes. 25 August 2006.

Hunter, James. *The Fiddle Music of Scotland*. Edinburgh: T.A. Constable Ltd., 1979: xi.

Jewell, Marianne. (Interview). August 2006. Scotsville, NS.

Johnston, Rev A.A. *A History of the Catholic Church in Eastern Nova Scotia Vol. 1- 1611-1827*. Antigonish: St. Francis Xavier University Press, 1971.

Johnston, Rev A.A. *A History of the Catholic Church in Eastern Nova Scotia Vol. 2- 1827-1880*. Antigonish: St. Francis Xavier University Press, 1971.

Kennedy, Brendon. "Island Musicians to Teach at Celtic Music School." *Cape Breton Post* 6 April, 1996.

King, Nancy. "Inverness County Hoping to Feature Road Signs in Both Gaelic and English." *Cape Breton Post* 8 Dec. 2006: A3.

King, Nancy. "Irish Singer Returns to Cape Breton to Explore Island's Culture and Music." *Cape Breton Post* 15 June 2005: B9.

Lamb, Tila. (Conversation). July 2006. Big Pond, NS.

LeBlanc, Alfred. "The Reel Thing." *Equinox* Sept./Oct. 1994:61-64.

"Louis Destroys Schmeling in Rematch." The International Boxing Hall of Fame. <http://www.ibhof.com/ibhfhvy5.htm> (20 Dec. 1999).

Luther, Mark. Founder and Director of Rocky Mountain Fiddle Camp, Colorado. Email to The Author. June 2007. [www.rmfiddle.com]

MacDonald, Alexander. "Cape Breton Fiddle Music, Is It Unique? Yes! What Makes It So?" *The Inverness Oran* July 1996: 12.

MacDonald, Angus. "In Defence of Scotland's Piping – Dr. Angus Responds" *The Clansman*. December/January, 1991/1992.

MacDonald, Donnie. (Interview). July 13, 2006. East Bay, NS.

MacDonald, Francis. (Interview). July 16, 2006. Sydney, NS.

Macdonald, Frank. "Buddy MacMaster. Concert Celebrates 'Guy Who Kept Celtic Music Alive.'" *The Inverness Oran* 14 Oct. 1998: 9.

Macdonald, Frank. "Buddy MacMaster and Joey Beaton at Annual Cowboy Poetry Gathering." *The Inverness Oran* 27 Jan. 1999: 12-13.

Macdonald, Frank. "It's Doctor Buddy as CBU Honours A 'Very Special Man' in Judique." *The Inverness Oran*. 11 October 2006.

Macdonald, Frank. *Making A Difference. Inverness County 1900-2000.* Inverness Communications Ltd.: Summer 2000: 1

Macdonald, Frank. "Saluting the Master." *The Inverness Oran.* 12 October, 1994.

Macdonald, Frank. "Willie, Elizabeth and Buddy. Mabou Hosts Tribute to Three Cultural Greats." *The Inverness Oran* 4 March 1998: A1.

MacDonald, Janette. "Historical And Social Development of Judique Nova Scotia." Unpublished Essay. St. F.X. University. May 1968.

MacDonald-Magone, Barbara. (Interview). 2006. California, USA.

MacDonald, Mary Janet and Betty Matheson, et. al. *No Less No More Just Four on the Floor: A Guide to Teaching Traditional Cape Breton Square Sets for Public Schools.* Halifax: Dance Nova Scotia, 1992.

MacDonald, Mary Janet. (Interview). 21 August 2006. Port Hood, NS.

MacDonald, Murdoch Johnnie Archie. (Interview). 2006. Seattle, USA.

MacDonald, Norman, Scotland. E-mail to the author. (July 2006).

MacDonald, Premier Rodney. Acknowledgement of Buddy MacMaster's Honourary Degree. Cape Breton University Convocation. St Andrew's Church, Judique, NS. 9 October 2006.

MacDonald, Steve. "College of Cape Breton Heralds New Year with Live Ceilidh Broadcast to Scotland." *College Canada* 4.4 (April 1979).

MacDonald, Tracey. "New albums help revive Gaelic songs." *Cape Breton Post.* 2 May 1995: 21.

MacDonell, Margaret. Archive File at St. F. X. University. "Friends Honor Fiddler." *The Casket* 131.12. 24 November 1982.

MacDonell, Margaret. *The Emigrant Experience: Songs of Highland Emigrants of North America.* Toronto: University of Toronto Press, 1982: 59.

MacDougall, Jackie. (Interview). 2006. Judique, NS.

MacDougall, John L. *History of Inverness County, Nova Scotia.* Ontario: Mika Publication, 1972: 555.

MacEachen, Frances. "A Tribute to Dan Joe MacInnis: A Lifetime of Scottish Music." *The Clansman* Oct./Nov. 1991.

MacEachen, Frances. "Buddy – A Master Shares His Music." *The Clansman* June/July 1991: 8.

MacEachen, Frances. "Buddy MacMaster: A Master and His Craft." *The Reporter* 10 July 1991: 7.

MacEachen, Frances. "The Broad Cove Concert – The Best Gift of All." *The Clansman* Oct./Nov. 1991.

MacEachen, Rev. J.H. "The Broad Cove Concerts." *St. Margaret's Church 1857-1982: 125 Years.* Antigonish, NS: The Casket, 1982.

MacGillivray, Allister. *The Cape Breton Fiddler.* Sydney: City Printers Ltd., 1981: 150-151.

MacHattie, Marjorie. "A Visit with Ray 'Mac' MacDonald, In Honour of the 50th Year of CJFX Radio." *Cape Breton's Magazine* :75-92.

MacInnes, Sheldon. *A Journey in Celtic Music, Cape Breton Style.* Sydney: University College of Cape Breton Press, 1997.

MacInnes, Sheldon. "Both Sides of the Water." *The Centre of the World at the Edge of a Continent.* Editors Carol Corbin and Judith Rolls. Sydney: University College of Cape Breton Press, 1996.

MacInnis, Christie. (Conversation). June 2006. Big Pond, NS.

MacInnis, Frank. (Interviews and conversations). 1999-2007. Creignish, NS.

MacInnis, Jimmy and Margie. (Interview). 2006. Mabou, NS.

MacInnis, J.J. "Violin Players I Have Met." *Eilean Cheap Breatann, Volumes I and II* 1943-44.

MacIntyre, Linden. E-mail to the author. 27 October 2006.

MacIntyre, Linden. "Evening of Merriment, and Tension." *Chronicle Herald*, 1975.

MacIntyre, Sandy. "Fiddling Cape Breton Style." *Fiddler Magazine* Summer 1996.

MacIsaac, Ashley. *Fine thank you very much.* Ancient Music. 1996.

MacIsaac, Ashley with Francis Condron. *Fiddling with Disaster.* Toronto, ON: Warwick Publishing, 2003.

MacKinnon, Ian. *Fiddling to Fortune: the Role of Commercial Recordings Made by Cape Breton Fiddlers in the Fiddle Music Tradition of Cape Breton Island.* M.A. Diss. Memorial University, 1989.

MacKinnon, Lorrie. (Interview). 13 August 2006. Inverness, NS.

MacLellan, Malcolm. *The Glen "An Gleann's An Robh Mi Og."* Antigonish, NS: Casket Printing and Publishing Co., Ltd., 1982.

MacLeod, Allan, Scotland. E-mail to the author. July 2006.

MacMaster, Buddy. Feature Story – Ceilidh Trail School of Music. *1st Edition*. CBC Halifax Archive: Tape # BP-5455. 12 August 1996.

MacMaster, Buddy. Feature Story – *Saturday Morning Show*. (25 May 1985). CBC Radio Collection. Nova Scotia Archives and Records Management: Location #Ar 3762-3764.

MacMaster, Buddy. Feature Story – Helen Creighton Award. *CBC News at Six*. CBC Halifax Archive: Tape # XP-8141. 28 February 2006.

MacMaster, Buddy. Feature Story – Order of Canada Award. *1st Edition*. CBC Halifax Archive: Tape # BP-6892. 14 July 2000.

MacMaster, Buddy. Feature Story – Order of Nova Scotia Award. *Canada Now NS*. CBC Halifax Archive: Tape # XP-7648. 21 October 2003.

MacMaster, Buddy. *Glencoe Hall*. Cassette. 1991.

MacMaster, Buddy. Interview with Bobby MacEachern. CIGO Radio – 101.5 The Hawk, Port Hawkesbury. July 2000.

MacMaster, Buddy. Interview with John Cable. *Radio Noon* – CBC Radio. (25 June 1984). Nova Scotia Archives and Records Management: Location # AR 4465.

MacMaster, Buddy. Interview with Jim Nunn. CBC Halifax Archive: Tape # XP-7921. 18 October 2004.

MacMaster, Buddy. Interview with Jim Nunn. CBC Halifax Archive: Tape # BP-3494. 28 December 1992.

MacMaster, Buddy. Interview with Joey Beaton. 6 October 1993.

MacMaster, Buddy. Interview with Joey Beaton. 30 March 1998.

MacMaster, Buddy. Interview with Linda Kelly. CBC Halifax Archive: Tape # BP-5939. 1997 October 16.

MacMaster, Buddy. (Interviews). 1999-2006. Judique, NS.

MacMaster, Buddy. *The Judique Flyer*. Steve MacDonald. 2002.

MacMaster, Buddy. *Judique on The Floor*. Record Album. Mira: Seacape. 1989.

MacMaster, Buddy and Natalie MacMaster. *Natalie and Buddy MacMaster*. MacMaster Music Inc.: Halifax, NS. 2005.

MacMaster, Marie. (Conversation). June 2006. Judique, NS.

MacMaster, Natalie. *Natalie MacMaster Live*. MacMaster Music Inc.: Mississauga, ON and Glencoe Hall, NS. 2002.

MacMaster Sisters – Betty Lou Beaton, Lorraine MacDonnell, Genevieve Whalen, Jeannie Brennan. (Interview). October 2006.

MacNeil, Jack, Big Pond. E-mail to the author. 18 October 2006.

MacPhee, Doug. (Interview). 8 November 2006. New Waterford, NS.

"The Master of the Cape Breton Fiddle. Buddy MacMaster to Be Subject of CBC Documentary." *The Inverness Oran* 19 Apr. 1995: 15.

Mathieson, Kenny. *Celtic Music*. San Francisco, CA: Backbeat Books, 2001.

Matheson, Betty. (Interview). July 2006. Dominion, NS.

Melhuish, Martin. *Celtic Tides – Traditional Music in a New Age*. Ontario: Quarry Press Inc., 1998.

Moore, Maggie. "Scottish Step Dancing." Augusta Heritage Center Program, July 23-28, 1995: 67-73.

Morris, Rev. Angus. (Interview). 15 August 2006. Mabou, NS.

Morris, Rev. Eugene. (Interview). 14 July 2006. Port Hood, NS.

Municipal Council Minutes 1968-1975. Retrieved from the Clerk's Office, Municipality of the County of Inverness, April 2003 and July-August 2006.

Murphy, Peter. "Buddy Master of the Fiddle!" *The Cape Bretoner* Summer 2000: 36-38.

Murray, Sonny. (Interview). 2006. Sydney Forks, NS.

"New Video Features Fiddler Buddy MacMaster." *The Casket* 2 Dec. 1992.

Nova Scotia. *This is Nova Scotia, Canada's Seacoast: 2006 Doers' & Dreamers' Guide*. Halifax: Nova Scotia Tourism, Culture and Heritage, p. 171.

"Queens Hall Sell-Out." *Box and Fiddle* [Scotland] Oct. 1984.

Randall, Janine. (Interview). 29 November 2006. Boston, USA.

Raytel Photo Caption in *The Cape Breton Highlander* 13 July 1966: 18.

Schoultz, Bob. "Cameo of a Scottish Fiddler: Buddy MacMaster of Cape Breton." (Date N/A).

Shaw, John. Liner Notes. *The Music of Cape Breton: Volume II – Cape Breton Scottish Fiddle*. Record Album. Topic Records, 12TS353, 1978.

Skinner, James Scott. *My Life and Adventures*. Scotland: Wallace Music, 1994.

"Spring Convocation Set for May 7. St. F.X. to Confer 5 Honorary Degrees." *The Casket* 26 Apr. 1995: A1.

St. Clair, Jim, Mull River, NS. E-mail to the author. August 2006.

St. Clair, Jim. "Tribute to Intercolonial Railway – Via Rail." CBC-AM Radio. 15 Jan. 1990.

Stecher, Jody. "Buddy MacMaster: Master Fiddler from Cape Breton." *Strings: The Magazine for Players and Makers of Bowed Instruments* Jan./Feb. 1992: 31-34.

Stecher, Jody. (Interview). 2006. California, USA.

Stephens, David E. *Iron Roads – Railroads of Nova Scotia*. Windsor, Nova Scotia: Lancelot Press, 1972.

The Casket. September 17, 1891.

"The Vanishing Cape Breton Fiddler." Produced and Narrated by Ron MacInnis. CBC-TV, Halifax. 1971.

Thompson, Alexa. "The Judique Flyer. Buddy MacMaster, Order of Canada." *Celtic Heritage* Sept./Oct. 2000: 4-5.

Thompson, Derick S., ed. *The Companion to Gaelic Scotland*. Oxford, England: Basil Blackwell Ltd., 1983: 7.

Thompson, Marie. *The Fall and Rise of The Cape Breton Fiddler: 1955-1982*. MA. Diss. St. Mary's University, 2003.

"Tony Galento." *Wikipedia, The Free Encyclopedia*. Online. http://en.wikipedia.org/wiki/Tony_Galento (retrieved 21 June 2005).

Wade-Matthews, Max. *Music, An Illustrated History*. London: Hermes House, 2001.

White, Fred, Big Pond, NS. E-mail to the author. (2006).